For the librarian, lawyer, business historian, and researcher
in records of the people of old New York

I0126524

Guide to
Genealogical and Biographical Sources
for New York City (Manhattan)
1783 - 1898

by

ROSALIE FELLOWS BAILEY, A.B., F.A.S.G.

With INTRODUCTION by
JOHN ROSS DELAFIELD, LL.B., D.S M.

with NEW INTRODUCTION by
HARRY MACY, JR., F.A.S.G.

CLEARFIELD

NEW INTRODUCTION

Rosalie Fellows Bailey (1908–1991), the first woman Fellow of The American Society of Genealogists, devoted her life to genealogy and particularly to New York genealogy. Her *Pre-Revolutionary Dutch Houses and Families in Northern New Jersey and Southern New York* (New York: William Morrow & Co., 1936, reprinted by Dover Books, 1968) and *Dutch Systems in Family Naming, New York–New Jersey* (Washington: National Genealogical Society, 1953) are still standard references. She also was the author of articles in *The New York Genealogical and Biographical Record* and other journals.

Miss Bailey's years of research in New York City records made her realize the need for a comprehensive research guide for post-Revolutionary New York City. The result was the present guide, first published as an article in *The New England Historical and Genealogical Register*, vols. 106–108 (1952–54) and then reprinted with additions in book form in 1954. Since then, it has been an essential research tool for the serious student of 19th-century New York City genealogy, history, and biography.

The first section of the guide covers the period from the end of the American Revolution in 1783 to 1855. The second section (beginning on page 66) covers the years 1855–1898, with additions for the earlier period. The geographic area covered by the guide is the present Borough of Manhattan, or New York County. Miss Bailey did not attempt to include the equally numerous resources for the other boroughs of the city; namely, The Bronx (annexed in two stages, in 1874 and 1895) and Brooklyn, Queens, and Staten Island (all annexed on January 1, 1898).

More than forty years have passed since this guide was written, and they have been extraordinary years for American genealogy. The landscape described by Miss Bailey has changed dramatically and almost always for the better. Anyone who uses this guide must be aware of these changes to avoid being misled by some of Miss Bailey's statements.

The resources described in the guide may be divided into two broad categories: printed works and manuscripts available in New York City libraries and unpublished original records of government and other institutions. The first category is the easier to deal with since all of the books and manuscripts described by Miss Bailey are still available, and in almost every case they are available at the same libraries she describes. On page 3, Miss Bailey lists five principal libraries which she subsequently refers to by their acronyms. It will be useful for the reader to know the current addresses of these libraries:

LIHS Formerly Long Island Historical Society, now Brooklyn Historical Society, 128 Pierrepont Street, Brooklyn, NY 11201.

NYGB New York Genealogical and Biographical Society, 122 East 58th Street, New York, NY 10022.

NYHS New-York Historical Society, 170 Central Park West, New York, NY 10024.

NYPL New York Public Library, Fifth Avenue at 42nd Street, New York, NY 10018.

NYSL New York State Library, Cultural Education Center, 7th Floor, Albany, NY 12230

New titles published since 1954 may be found in the same libraries. For these new publications researchers should examine ongoing indexes to historical and genealogical literature, such as *America: History and Life* (for historical titles) and *PERSI (Periodical Source Index*, for genealogical periodicals). Genealogists should pay particular attention to New York City articles and book reviews published in *The New York Genealogical and Biographical Record, The NYG&B Newsletter,* and *Dorot* (the journal of the Jewish Genealogical Society). For manuscripts acquired or catalogued since 1954, consult the ongoing *National Union Catalog of Manuscript Collections (NUCMC)*. Arthur J. Breton's *A Guide to the Manuscript Collections of the New-York Historical Society* (1972) adds many items to those noted by Miss Bailey. The *Guide to Historic Resources in New York County (Manhattan)*, 7 vols. (1988–90), though incomplete, covers holdings of several city institutions which Miss Bailey did not include in her guide.

From 1953 to 1967 Miss Bailey was a staff member of the Local History and Genealogy Division of the New York Public Library. The Division has a copy of the guide which Miss Bailey annotated with corrections and additions.

Many researchers will find Miss Bailey's description of printed and manuscript resources to be her most valuable contribution because no other guide to New York City genealogical research has dealt with these resources so comprehensively. Over and over again the careful researcher will find in her bibliographies an obscure title which holds information found in no other source. Thorough research in the 19th-century city cannot be done without reference to this part of the guide.

When we turn to the other broad category of material, the original records of government and other institutions, the scene has changed so drastically since 1954 that one may question whether Miss Bailey's guide still has any relevance in this area. The records she describes do in most cases still exist, and often her descriptions of them can be helpful. It is her statements regarding the availability and accessibility of these records that have become obsolete.

Since 1954 the Federal, State, County, and City governments have opened to the public a vast collection of records that were formerly inaccessible for research. In New York City these records are available through the following archives:

National Archives - Northeast Region, 201 Varick Street, New York, NY 10014 Originals or copies of many of the 19th-century federal records described by Miss Bailey are now at this facility, including census population schedules, passenger lists for the port of New York, the consolidated naturalizations index (to 1906), and naturalization records of the U.S. District Court for the Southern District of New York.

New York State Archives, Cultural Education Center, 11th Floor, Albany, NY 12230 The 19th-century records which in 1954 were in the custody of the Clerk of the Court of Appeals, Adjutant General, and other state officials are now at this repository. The State Archives also has original wills and will libers formerly at the New York County Surrogate's Court (or Surrogate's Office), but that Court retains its other records. Copies of some holdings of the State Archives are available on film at the National Archives, Northeast Region.

Division of Old Records, County Clerk's Office, New York County, 31 Chambers Street, Room 703, New York, NY 10007 The holdings of this facility have been expanded to include all records which Miss Bailey describes as being in the custody of the County Clerk.

Municipal Archives of the City of New York, 31 Chambers Street, Room 103, New York, NY 10007. Most 19th-century records which in 1954 were in the custody of the Department of Health, City Clerk, Comptroller, and other city offices are now in these archives. The most significant holdout is the Office of the City Register in the same building, which retains deeds, mortgages, and related land records described by Miss Bailey.

(31 Chambers Street, Manhattan, is the building which Miss Bailey refers to as the Hall of Records. In addition to the Municipal Archives and City Register, it houses the New York County Surrogate's Court and the County Clerk's Division of Old Records. All are open to the public.)

A large percentage of New York City Records have now been microfilmed. Most of the films were made by the Genealogical Society of Utah and are available at the Family History Library of the Church of Jesus Christ of Latter-day Saints in Salt Lake City and at LDS Family History Centers worldwide. Researchers outside of New York City thus have easy access to many of the records described by Miss Bailey. Copies of many of the same films are also available at libraries and archives in New York City.

With all these changes, the need for an updated guide, particularly for government records, was recognized by the Jewish Genealogical Society, which in 1989 published *Genealogical Resources in the New York Metropolitan Area*, edited by Estelle Guzik (and referred to as "the JGS guide"). While Miss Bailey approaches the records by categories (probate, land, naturalization, etc.), the JGS guide presents the same material by repositories, both government and private, and gives detailed instructions for the use of each facility in addition to describing its holdings. Reflecting another change in American genealogy since 1954, the JGS guide also extends its coverage well into the 20th century. No one should attempt to do 19th-century New York City research without Miss Bailey's guide, but it should be used in conjunction with the JGS guide. At the present writing, the 1989 edition of the JGS guide is still in print, and a revised edition is planned. Until the revised edition appears, researchers will find that changes since 1989 affecting New York City records have been chronicled in the issues of *Dorot* and *The NYG&B Newsletter.*

Genealogical research in New York City has been described as "notoriously difficult," usually by commentators who view the city from afar. While research in this huge city is very different from research in rural or small-town America, a city of this size also has a far greater number of sources to utilize, sources which are often immense in size. Armed with Miss Bailey's guide and other research aids, the diligent genealogist can learn how to make use of this rich store of genealogical and historical material.

New York, 1997
Harry Macy, Jr., F.A.S.G.
Associate Editor, *The New York Genealogical and Biographical Record*

ACKNOWLEDGMENTS

This Guide to Sources could not have achieved its present fullness and form without the suggestions and encouragement of Dr. Arthur Adams, President of The American Society of Genealogists and Editor of the *New England Historical and Genealogical Register*, and Miss Elsie McCormack, assistant editor of this quarterly in which the main text of this Guide was initially published; also Miss Dorothy Barck, Librarian of The New-York Historical Society, Miss Marie Becker, reference librarian of the latter society, and my fellow staff members of The New York Public Library; also, last but not least, Dr. Milton Halsey Thomas, Curator of Columbiana at Columbia University, Miss Edna Jacobsen, Associate Librarian of The New York State Library, and Meredith B. Colket, Jr., of the General Reference Section, National Archives. My thanks and appreciation are profusely extended to them.

ROSALIE FELLOWS BAILEY.

New York, N. Y.
January 24, 1954

INTRODUCTION

When one is by good fortune permitted to devote her entire lifetime to the subject of her enthusiasm, makes it her life work, and brings to it high intellectual ability and training, together with unusual energy and perseverance, something of unusual excellence is assured. This guide is such a work. Though the region covered by it is limited, it is in its field one of the most important, perhaps the most important, in the United States. Through the portal of New York City and from the teeming millions of its people and great accumulation of wealth, have come, in large part, the prosperity and even in some measure the character of our people. To be able to trace the backgrounds of these people and their history is therefore of first importance.

There are, of course, the never ending imaginary claims,, such as the Anneke Jans case. But these are not the important cases in life. The real problems of ancestry and descent are those that come up in establishing legal rights. These can and often are solved through accurate research and without litigation. Such a case, though in Virginia and not in New York, was the establishing of the right of Albert Fairfax of Virginia to the Scottish barony of Fairfax. This required proof for five generations. Where litigation becomes necessary, these documents are in good part legal evidence, admissible in court, and the only proofs that exist.

Miss Bailey out of practical experience and able study and research for many years has written and had published this guide. It covers the most difficult and most important period of the past of the people of New York City. Those who could help from personal recollection and with hearsay clues are now mostly dead.

And, but for the documents, printed and manuscript, which Miss Bailey has so well classified and described, what they knew has passed with them.

A dip into the mass of records Miss Bailey has catalogued will soon make one aware that knowledge of them alone will not quickly bring results. Experience and skill are needed to make the best use of this information. The presentation of it as it is given in this guide, however, will give reasonable hope that any problem within its limits of time and place may be solved.

JOHN ROSS DELAFIELD, LL.B.

New York, N. Y.
February 8, 1954

CONTENTS

GUIDE TO GENEALOGICAL AND BIOGRAPHICAL SOURCES FOR NEW YORK CITY: 1783–1855*

By ROSALIE FELLOWS BAILEY, of New York City
Fellow of The American Society of Genealogists

New York City, for a short time the capital of the new nation, attracted so many Yankee traders and shippers among others as to triple[1] its population between 1786 and 1805 and become the leading port of the nation by 1823, in which year its custom-house duties slightly exceeded the combined total for Boston, Philadelphia, Baltimore, Norfolk, and Savannah.[2] And then, with the opening of the Erie Canal in 1825, the city mushroomed as the gateway to the West. Because of the rapid immigration to New York City from many regions, because of the unusual difficulties of searching in this period and the special kinds of source material to be used, and because of the importance of a newly available series of records,[3] this Guide has been compiled for old New York City (Manhattan Island).

The half century or so following the Revolution is often the most difficult period in America for which to find first-class proof of a lineage. I say this with due respect for the special difficulties presented in the New Netherland of the 1600's before surnames were established as we know them today. There seem to be four basic factors rendering that era so difficult to bridge with first-class genealogical proof.

First, it is the in-between period, later than most published records (which for the New York area often run to the Revolution or 1800) and earlier than most family accounts or the recollections or those now or recently living, also earlier than obituary sketches and good vital statistics (which for New York City and State are based on laws of 1853 and 1880 respectively).

Secondly, it is the period in which a considerable percentage of families moved about in the new nation. New York City had no Western Reserve or Shenandoah Valley and Cumberland Gap funneling the direction of these movements, and it is often difficult even to guess whence a recently arrived New Yorker came. Incidentally, in New York City the population change had started under the British Army occupation of the Revolutionary War years.

---

*The compiler of this guide is a professional genealogical researcher, author of *Pre-Revolutionary Dutch Houses and Families in Northern New Jersey and Southern New York* and of numerous genealogical articles. Her work has led her into varied fields, including tracing unknown heirs under the laws of New York (which differentiate between cousins of the blood and by adoption) with the result that this guide includes unusual sources. — Editor.

[1] Little-known statistical censuses in *Census of the Electors and Total Population of the City and County of New York,* 1807, pamphlet at NYPL.

[2] *Evening Post,* issue of January 8, 1824, p. 2.

[3] Death records of New York City, starting 1801 — originals not open to the public.

1

Thirdly, it is a period of tremendous population growth. While New York City had always been cosmopolitan in character (having about 4 or 500 men of 18 different languages in 1643, with preaching in Dutch and French as early as 1628[4]), it grew from a city in 1786 of 23,614 inhabitants with upper development at about Chambers and Hester Streets to a city in 1850 of 515,547 inhabitants with upper development at about 42nd Street.[5] (The populous area is to be distinguished from the city's bounds, which by 1730 charter surrounded the entire Manhattan Island and small adjoining islands and by 1897 charter were extended to form the present Greater New York City.) As a result of such population growth, many unrelated adults bore the same name at the same time. Even such an unusual masculine name as Florence McCarthy was borne by two contemporary men. The searcher must therefore multiply his proofs to be sure he is using only those records applying to the person in whom he is interested.

Fourthly, it is a period presenting with respect to its cities' records the double-barrelled problem of great volume and of general inaccessibility. For New York City, relatively few nineteenth century records have been copied, let alone published, yet because the city grew so fast in population and developed area, the churches, for instance, multiplied from 22 in 1789 to 150 in 1837,[6] and such increase was only the beginning. The searcher cannot obtain access to many records (nor is the custodian usually in a position to make the detailed search that may be desirable); those records that are accessible take a considerable time to search because of their great volume and the many people bearing the name in which he is interested.

And perhaps we should add a *fifth* factor — that many families changed their religious affiliation in this period.

Getting started is a very real genealogical problem in the New York City of about 1800 as a result of the factors just mentioned. Usually time must be spent in gathering sufficient leads with which to start serious research. The searcher is aided in covering the groundwork by the increasing number of abstracts of wills and of newspaper marriage and death notices, but he is cautioned that all abstracts have errors and omissions so that he should verify any questionable or important point by the original. Often, much preliminary work may be avoided if a pertinent early New York City death record is located, because this usually points to less than a handful of churches that existed at the time and place of the deceased's birth.

The best collections of material are at the following libraries; mention of a library (by initials) will be confined to items that

4 *Narratives of New Netherland 1609-1664*, J. F. Jameson, 1909, pp. 88, 125, 259.

5 Statistics from early censuses in *Census of the State of New-York for 1855*, Franklin B. Hough, 1857, pp. viii & xxiv; *The Kip Family in America*, p. 94

6 *The City of New York in . . 1789*, Thomas E. V. Smith, 1889, p. 125; *New-York as it is, in 1837*, pr. J. Disturnell, 1837, p. 120.

might not be generally available and to classes of records in which it is outstanding.

LIHS   Long Island Historical Society, Clinton and Pierrepont Sts., Brooklyn, N. Y.

NYGB   New York Genealogical and Biographical Society, 122 East 58 St., New York, N. Y.

NYHS   The New-York Historical Society, 77th St. and Central Park West, New York, N. Y.

NYPL   New York Public Library, 42nd St. and Fifth Ave., New York, N. Y.

NYSL   The New York State Library, Albany 1, N. Y. (Manuscripts and History Section).

The source material in this seventy-year period may be thus classified in these groups — listed for the most part in the likely order of research, assuming an average amount of vague knowledge or assumptions.

A.   The Man or Woman
  1. Probate and related records
  2. Death notices
  3. Death records

B.   The Wife and her Father
  4. Printed deed indexes
  5. Marriage notices
  6. Means of identifying the church of a minister

C.   Casting for Clues
  7. Directories
  8. Name lists and biographical sketches by occupation

  9. Other name lists: education, membership, wealth, etc.
  10. Secondary and other sources

D.   The Non-native New Yorker
  11. Origin
  12. Passage and naturalization

E.   Various Aids
  13. State and federal censuses
  14. Maps, street and land records
  15. Burial records and cemeteries
  16. Military records
  17. Special records and archives: civil, vital, change of name, newspaper, etc.
  18. Church records.

PROBATE AND RELATED RECORDS

For New York County, which is the New York City of the genealogist,[7] the basic material is at the Office of the Surrogate's Court of the County of New York on Chambers Street. But other courts also have material relating to estates and heirs.

Two early laws materially changed inheritance in New York, the eldest son no longer having special privileges. The law of 1786 (Chap. 27) abolished entail and that of 1787 (Chap. 38) established the distribution of an intestate estate (net) as one-half to the widow with residue in *equal* portions among the children (with some modifications to ensure equality). The latter law also stipulated that administration on an intestate estate should be granted to the widow or next of kin of the deceased if any of them would accept.

---

[7] Population movements often render advisable a search also of Surrogate's records of the adjoining counties: Kings, Queens, and Richmond (all now in Greater New York City but still having their own Surrogate's Offices) and Westchester. The latter county is not part of the city except for its southern end which, added to New York County in 1874 and 1895, was organized into Bronx County 1914.

The Court of Probates was organized by law of 1778 (Chap. 12) to replace the Prerogative Court; it moved from New York to Albany in 1799 and was abolished in 1823. It had jurisdiction when the deceased had effects in more than one county, while a Surrogate had power at first only over estates exclusively in his county.[8] A law of May 1784 permitted appeal to the Court of Probates within 18 months of this law from the probates made 1776–1783 under British rule of the Southern District of the state,[9] otherwise confirming them. The law of 1787 establishing county Surrogates did *not* give them exclusive jurisdiction and it specifically restricted to the Court of Probates all probate and administration when persons died out of the state and when non-residents died within the state. Under the 1799 law, jurisdiction over the latter two kinds of estates was shared with the Surrogate of the appropriate county; the Revised Statutes of 1813 confirmed this, and also stated that the Surrogate had exclusive power to prove wills of the inhabitants of his county. The same law of 1787 (Chap. 38) gave to the Court of Probates a new power (not held under British custom) to call administrators and executors to account, including power to decree and settle order of distribution and to enforce its decrees. The 1786 law (Chap. 27) for the relief of creditors gave authority to the Court of Probates, in cases of deficiency in the personal estate, to order sale of real estate to pay debts, an authority shared to a limited extent with the Surrogate under the 1799 law. The Court of Probates had appellate jurisdiction over the county Surrogates 1787–1823.

The old Supreme Court (1683–1847) and the Court of Common Pleas had accumulated powers not conferred on Surrogates as development of a 1743 law and a similar law passed 1789 (Chap. 1), for the more speedy recovery of legacies. It entitled heirs to sue executors or administrators for an accounting in the Supreme Court or any other court of record in the state. The law of 1786 (Chap. 27) provided that any will devising real estate could be brought for probate before the inferior Court of Common Pleas of the county in which was the real estate, or if the lands were in several counties, before the Supreme Court. The Supreme Court and the Court of Common Pleas thus had the power of compelling executors to account and both courts proved wills of real estate — until the Revised Statutes of 1829. The practice of accounting in the Prerogative Court had fallen into disuse in colonial times because the above act and the general jurisdiction exercised by the Court of Chancery in such cases furnished a more effectual remedy. Hence any settlement, distribution, and accounting records for estates before 1829 would appear, if they exist, among the voluminous and hard-to-use records of one of these courts (or perhaps of the Court of Probates).

---

[8] This division of jurisdiction given by Judge Daly must be a carryover of colonial practice, because the 1778 law merely states that the Court of Probates is to have all powers and authorities and like jurisdiction of the Prerogative Court except for appointing Surrogates. The text of this section of the Guide is based largely on the Daly and Vosburgh references listed below and on my study of laws of New York for 1778–1799.

[9] The Southern District was all south and east of Westchester County's north border.

4

The Court of Chancery was a court of equity, abolished in 1847. I am not too familiar with its records or its powers over estates and heirs. A 1788 law (Chap. 12) concerning idiots, lunatics, and infant trustees permitted conveyance of lands by direction of the Court of Chancery. Among this court's libers of the 1790's, I have seen such items as (1) an order to pay specified sums to a remarried woman for herself and also as mother of her infant children by a previous husband (all named) for support during their minority and (2) a petition of infants aged 14 yrs. 8 mos. and 12 yrs. 8 mos. to have their mother's last husband appointed guardian during their minority, describing the farm left by their father of whom they are the only children, and giving names and residences of all except the mother who is mentioned as also dead. In 1802 Surrogates were authorized to appoint guardians for infants as fully as the Chancellor might do, and the latter continued to concern himself at least with infants' petitions to sell real estate. Wills could be proved before the Court of Chancery in limited instances, according to a Law of 1830 (Chap. 320). Appellate jurisdiction over Surrogate decisions was vested in the Court of Chancery 1823–1847. The various functions of the Court of Chancery were transferred to the Supreme Court at the latter's reorganization in 1847.

There had been Surrogates in some counties occasionally before 1787, but the basic law establishing the present system of Surrogate's Courts went into effect May 1, 1787 (Chap. 38). This law authorized appointment of a Surrogate for each county, who was empowered to probate wills and grant letters of administration for estates of those who died in the county or who were inhabitants of it but died while absent on a business journey. The law of 1799 (Chap. 64) enlarged this to include power over those estates that in 1787 had been restricted to the Court of Probates. This 1799 law empowered the Surrogate to prove wills of real estate and to order sale of real estate to pay debts, in both instances only when the estate's lands were confined to his county, and he could appoint guardians for infants merely for such real estate sales; his powers over real estate were enlarged 1806–1810. In 1802 he was given power to appoint guardians for infants. The Revised Statutes of 1813 (Chap. 79) stated he had exclusive power to prove wills of inhabitants of his county regardless of place of death. The Revised Statutes of 1829 (Chap. 6) stated that any will devising real estate could be brought before the Surrogate of the county to whom the probate of the testator's will would belong, and that the Surrogate had sole and exclusive power within his county to prove wills so far as they related to personal property.

The Surrogate's Office of New York County has complete sets of libers, except for the missing volume 1 of letters of administration (covering a few years before Feb. 14, 1784). As to papers of the early laws including the Revised Laws of 1813 specified that the will might be returned to executor or family after recording. The New York Surrogate's files of papers are full and complete only after about 1845, despite an 1829 law specifying that the

5

Surrogate had to keep on file affidavits, petitions, etc. Of these, the most important to the genealogist is usually the petition or citation listing all the next of kin, often giving the exact relationship and sometimes exact addresses. The 1786 law requiring that notice be given to heirs before offering a will for probate either was not followed or did not result in such early papers being kept. Many early inventories are known to have been thrown away when the office moved about 1902 to its present quarters. The 1799 law required that probate books and papers for the Southern District of the state prior to May 1, 1787 be turned over to the Surrogate of New York County, but many papers of such eighteenth century estates are now with the Clerk of the Court of Appeals at Albany.

Nature, Extent and History of the Jurisdiction of the Surrogates' Courts of the State of New York, Judge Charles Patrick Daly, 1863.

"Surrogates' Courts and Records in the Colony and State of New York, 1664–1847", Royden W. Vosburgh, in N. Y. Hist'l Ass'n *Quarterly Journal,* April 1922, pp. 105–16.

"Early New York Probate Records at the Hall of Records, Chambers St., Manhattan", Rosalie Fellows Bailey, in NYGB *Record,* v. 81, pp. 44–47.

Index of Wills for (should read: on file at) New York County 1662–1850, 1851–1875, MS by Ray C. Sawyer.

Index of Letters of Administration filed in New York County 1743–1875, MS by Gertrude Barber.

"Abstracts of Wills" in NYHS *Collections,* 1892–1908 (covers wills and administrations for 1665–1800; inaccurate).

Abstracts of Wills for New York County 1801–1855, MS by Sawyer and Barber at NYPL and LIHS.

Above indexes and abstracts concern only records now at New York County Surrogate's Office.

Reports of Cases argued and determined in the Surrogate's Court of the County of New York, Alexander W. Bradford, in 2 vols., 1851 and 1854.

Records in the New York County Surrogate's Office, Hall of Records, Chambers St., primarily: Administration bonds 1742–1828, 1835–1926; Letters of administration 1743–1927; Guardianship bond books 1802–1927; Guardians accounts 1837–1898; Record of Dower 1831–1857; Inventories of Property 1776–1786, 1793–1865; Wills 1665–1927; Letters testamentary 1830–1927; Renunciation of executors 1831–1914; Orders for citation 1851–1872; Proceedings in the sale of real estate 1800–1927; Proceedings to probate wills of real estate 1830–1874 (file for each estate may include misc. items).

New York County Surrogate's Office's first 56 libers of wills (1665–1823) lithographed 1870–71; sheets for about 40 of these libers at NYHS, with MS index for 1801–1823.

Inventories of estates in the Southern District of New York, 610 original papers 1717–1844 at NYHS, including 79 after 1800; for lists before 1800 see NYHS *Quarterly Bulletin,* v. 6 and v. 8.

Intestate Estates 1831 to date[10] settled by the Public Administrator for New York County, Dep't of Finance, Room 309, Hall of Records, Chambers St., New York, N. Y.

Index to Wills proved in Supreme Court (at N. Y. C. and Albany), *Court of Common Pleas, County Court and Court of Probates, and on file in Office of Clerk of Court of Appeals,* John J. Post, 1899, at LIHS and NYHS (concerns wills affecting real estate in Greater N. Y. C. not on record in Surrogate's Offices of the counties of Greater N. Y. C.).

<hr />

[10] Stokes, VI:199 gives these records as starting 1802, with gaps; the official gave me 1831.

Abstracts of Wills probated at Common Pleas Court, N. Y. C. 1819–1892 and at Supreme Court for New York County 1821–1829, 1847–1870, MS by Ray C. Sawyer 1948, at NYGB and LIHS.

Wills recorded in Supreme Court 1787–1829, 1847–1883 and in Court of Common Pleas 1805–1829, 1886–1892: in 7 libers with card index at New York County Clerk's Office, Room 703, Hall of Records, Chambers St., New York, N. Y. Papers of these courts also there.

Index to Wills of New York State 1653–1815 copied by Wm. A. D. Eardely dec'd and typed 1941, MS at LIHS and NYGB (includes Court of Chancery wills and Court of Probates files and wills and also some of its administrations 1787–1815 but not v. 1: 1778–1797).

Calendar of Wills on file and recorded in the offices of the Clerk of the Court of Appeals, of the County Clerk at Albany, and of the Secretary of State, 1626–1836, Berthold Fernow, 1896.

Court of Probates records 1778–1823, now in custody of Clerk of the Court of Appeals, Eagle St., Albany, N. Y. (Letters of Administration v. 1 for 1778–1797, 215 pp. and vol. for 1815–1823 are nowhere else available by abstract or index).

Court of Chancery records, 1700–1847, registers, minute books (70 vols. in Albany and 68 vols. in N. Y. C.), order books, decrees, pleadings, depositions, and other papers, mostly indexed by chief plaintiff: partly with the Clerk of the Court of Appeals, Eagle St., Albany, and partly with the New York County Clerk, Chambers St., New York.

DEATH NOTICES

The approximate period of death is often determinable by the interval (1) between the dates of execution and of probate of a will or (2) between a name's disappearance from the directory and the possible appearance of a widow's name. Even without a clue, the many indexed series of death notices abstracted from newspapers should be searched. These notices give age and date of death; they seldom give a clue to the church (unless in a religious paper) since they merely give the address of the residence from which the funeral will start.

New York Evening Post: MS of marriages and deaths Nov. 1801–Dec. 1890, Gertrude Barber.

Christian Intelligencer: Ms of marriages and deaths 1830–1871, Ray C. Sawyer (paper of the Reformed Dutch Church).

Long Island Star: Master card index of marriages and deaths 1809–1845, at LIHS (Brooklyn newspaper which customarily listed many N. Y. C. deaths of the week previous, without giving exact deathdate).

New York Weekly Museum: Marriages and deaths 1789–1799 in Valentine's *Manual,* N. S. vols. 1–5 (1916–1921) (alphabetical from January 1797); also 1799–Nov. 1801 in indexed MS at NYHS (including issues missing from series in Valentine's *Manual*); also 1789–1796 in indexed MS at LIHS and NYGB; also 1795–1814 in unindexed MS from an incomplete file, in Riker Coll., v. 9, Box 18, at NYPL. Complete series of such notices is in preparation by Clarence S. Brigham of Amer. Antiquarian Society.

New York Commercial Advertiser: MS of marriages 1810–1814 at NYGB, also MS of marriages and deaths Oct. 1827–Dec. 1831 at NYHS; all unindexed.

New York Magazine: MS of marriages and deaths 1790–1794 from an incomplete file, in Riker Coll., v. 9, Box 18, at NYPL.

McClean's Independent Journal: Marriages and deaths 1785–1787 in *The Journal of American Genealogy,* Allaben, v. 2 (1922).

Small files of various early newspapers at LIHS: MSS of marriages and deaths, indexed, at LIHS.

7

DEATH RECORDS

The death records 1801–1865 of old New York City[11] often make it possible to pick up the clue necessary to begin genealogical research on both the recently arrived New Yorker and the native New Yorker. This is so because the items churchyard or burial, place of birth, and age in the death record point to the most logical series of church records to be first examined. The importance of this clue is obvious since the city had close to 65 churches in use in the period 1801–1814 and many more as the century progressed. The valuable angle of religion in these death records is developed later in the sections on Cemeteries and Church Records.

A study of the common letters B and C in Death Register No. 1 (1801–1814) — see condensed table below — shows that of the American-born outside the city, the three largest groups came, about equally, from New England, New Jersey, and New York, and that of the foreign-born the countries providing the most immigrant deaths were Ireland (by far the largest) and then (in descending order) England, Scotland, and France with its West Indian island refugees. The importance of the clue of birthplace, to be found in these death records, is obvious; seldom is there any other record of New Yorkers proving the *place* of out-of-town origin.

New York (City)	858	Long Island	30	Richmond	1	Geneva	1
Native	84	Marblehead	1	Rockland County	2	Germany	13
		Marlborough	1	Shrewsbury, N. J.	2	Great Britain	1
Albany	3	Maryland	3	Stanford, N. J.	1	Guadaloupe	2
Amawalk	1	Massachusetts	5	Staten Island	3	Halifax	2
Amboy, N. J.	1	Morrisania	1	Stillwater	1	Holland	1
America	21	Nantucket	5	Ulster County	5	Ireland	126
Baltimore	2	New Burg	1	Vermont	1	London	1
Block Island	1	New England	2	Virginia	8	Madeira	1
Boston	4	New Haven	1	Washington	1	Martinique	1
Charleston	1	New Jersey	31	Westchester	5	Port au Prince	1
Columbia	2	New London	3	White Plains	1	St. Croix	1
Connecticut	15	New Port, R. I.	1			St. Domingo	8
Delaware	2	New Providence	1	Aberdeen, Scotld	1	St. Johns, Nova Scotia	1
Dutchess County	2	New York State	4	Africa	10	St. Vincent	1
Fishkill	1	Norfolk, Va.	1	Bermuda	1	Saxony	1
Flushing, L. I.	1	North Carolina	1	Canada	1	Scotland	21
Fort Stanwix	1	Orange County	3	Cape Francois	1	Spain	3
Goshen	1	Peekskill	1	Curacao	1	Sweden	1
Hackensack	1	Pennsylvania	6	Denmark	1	Switzerland	1
Haverstraw	1	Philadelphia	9	East Indies	1	Wales	1
Horse Neck	1	Poughkeepsie	2	England	45	West Indies	4
Kingston	1	Queens County	1	France	7		
Lancaster	1	Rhode Island	2	French Flanders	1	Unstated [12]	209

The searcher aware of the poor life expectancy of the era can often speed his work by concentrating his search, first, on average-age periods. The official analysis of deaths reported for 1805–1809 says that two-fifths were aged 5 years and under while four-fifths were aged 50 years and under;[13] my tabulation for Register No. 1 is not dissimilar in results.

Continuous registration of deaths in the city, preceding that of other vital statistics by a half century, goes back to an ordinance

[11] Microfilm 1801–1865 at NYGB, available to searchers who are members of the NYGB. The City's vital records are not open to the public: see note 50 in this Guide.

[12] Unstated birthplaces are virtually limited to the first register, in its opening years.

[13] *A Comparative Statement of the Number of Deaths in the City of New-York during the Years 1804–5–6–7–8 and 1809*, Report of the City Inspector (1810).

of Oct. 26, 1801.[14] It required sextons or others in charge of burial places in the city to report burials weekly to the city. The city acted thus early as a means of studying possible health measures for controlling epidemics; perhaps because of this, the names of deceased for some early years were not permanently filed and probably deaths in the rural part of the city were seldom reported,[15] especially if buried in family cemetery on the farm. As late as 1837 the City Inspector stated he received no returns of those dying within the city limits when the interment was without the city.[16] Modern, fuller death records start in 1866; they are physicians' certiñcates and include *inter alia* length of time resident in the city and parents' birthplace.[17] The items entered before 1866 were: date of death, name, residence (street or hospital), age, birthplace, cemetery, disease,[18] remarks (seldom more than "A black" or name of attending physician).

A few comments will help in the use of Register No. 1, misleadingly entitled Aug. 1, 1798–May 25, 1814. It has entries[17] made irregularly and with large gaps for the period October 1801 to August 1808. Starting December 1811, registration (though incomplete) is continuous and chronological within each letter of the alphabet. The former group is not chronological, it has a few unexpected entries such as August 1798 for C, and its arrangement for the year 1802 is curious. Among its 1802 entries for June, October, and November are a few entries for October and November 1801 and for June and October 1803; the immediate return to the norm of 1802 is not always clearly marked. Occasionally the church name is incompletely entered, but it can be identified through the sexton's name. The searcher is warned that occasionally the date of burial rather than of death is entered (as can be seen if possible to compare with one of the rare newspaper death notices of this early period).

The Basic Pattern[19] for Each Letter in Register #1

1804 July (last week) and August (first week) — 0 to 4 entries.
1808 May through August.
1801 October and November — 0 to 5 entries.
1802 Entire year plus some Oct. and Nov. 1801 and June and Oct. 1803.
1803 Entire year (except September).
1804 January through July.
1811 December.
1812–1816 Entire years to end of space allotted to the letter.
1814 has the most letters' ending.

---

[14] *Minutes of the Common Council*, III:43, 289, 477, 576.

[15] My inference from the city's deaths as printed in two N. Y. C. Directories for 1815 and 1816/17, the heading there specifically excluding Bloomingdale and Harlem (the names for the west side and north end of Manhattan Island); and see comment in Cemeteries section of Guide.

[16] *Annual Report from the City Inspector, of the Interments in the City and County of New York showing their Age, Sex, Colour and Places of Nativity for the Year 1837; Also a Table of Deaths and the Different Diseases Since the Year 1804* (1838). At the Dep't of Health are separate registers of Bodies in Transit 1859–1894.

[17] For the new requirements and for statistics on names in the early archives, see *Annual Report of the Metropolitan Board of Health for 1866* (1867), pp. 1, 13 & appx pp. 41, 43, 48.

[18] For a convenient table of causes of death, see *Minutes of the Common Council*, VI:33, for 1804–1809.

[19] Including the first page of the register (dates obliterated by mending tape), which consists of 1804 and 1808 entries as I have proved by internal and external evidence.

The large gaps in the regular series of death records prior to 1812 render especially valuable the following special lists of those who died from yellow fever epidemics. An item from each is given here as an indication of what may be found. I am including special lists of names of those who died in the later yellow fever and cholera epidemics under the impression that they supplement the regular series of death records.

year	yellow fever deaths	total deaths in months of the epidemic	notes, records, and sources
1791	?	?	First occurrence of the fever in the city for about 40 years; see the 1795 and 1822 books listed below.
1793	?	?	Health Committee Minutes 1793–96, at NYHS (no names).
1795	718	732	*Brief Account of the Epidemical Fever which lately prevailed in the City of New York*, Matthew L. Davis, 1795, at NYPL. Item: Malachi Treat, physician of the port, William St. List of names, etc., but including dates, from Mayor Varick's papers, in NYGB *Record*, v. 81. See also addenda of this guide, p. 68.
1798	c.1,524	2,086	*Account of the Malignant Fever lately Prevalent in the City of New-York*, James Hardie, 1799, at NYGB, NYHS, NYPL. It lists all 2,086 burials in cemeteries Aug. 1–Nov. 13. Item: Abernethey, George, shoemaker & his son George aet 12, 33 Barclay St., born Scotland.
1799	360	?	For names, see addenda of this guide, p. 89.
1803	674	1,256	For names, see addenda of this guide, p. 89.
1805	302	934	*Account of the Malignant Fever which prevailed in the City of New-York during the Autumn of 1805*, James Hardie, 1805, at NYHS and NYPL. Items: Oct 7 Adams, Henry, cartman, 25 Garden, born Ireland; Sept 29 Allen, Elizabeth, daughter of Mathias, 75 Courtland, ae 26, born New Jersey.
1819	41	?	*Statement of the Occurrences During a Malignant Yellow Fever in the City of New-York in . . . 1819 with a list of cases . . . of sick persons*, 1819, at NYHS. It gives details of 66 cases, and if recovered or deathdate. Items: Mrs. Conlin, aided to remove to Newburgh where she had friends, returned & died at 58 Front St.; Dennis M'Mullen sent to hospital at Fort Stevens where he died Sept 17.
1820	c. 150	?	*Report of the Committee of The Medical Society of the City and County of New York . . . of the Epidemic Fever . . . in 1820* (1820). It gives figures but no names of deceased.
1822	254	1,236	*Account of the Yellow Fever, which occurred in the City of New-York in the Year 1822*, James Hardie, 1822, at NYHS and NYPL. It lists deaths of fever contracted in the city. Items: Aug. 26 Atkinson, Mary wife of Wm, from 47 Greenwich St., died at Marine Hospital; Aug 24 Baisely, Nicholas, who had been in the infected district, died at Brooklyn. *History of the Proceedings of the Board of Health of the City of New-York in . . . 1822; together with an Account of . . . the Yellow Fever*, 1823, at NYHS. Its table of yellow fever cases includes column of resi-

dence in or contracted in sickly districts and column of residence or removal out of sickly districts. Items (in part): Caroline Reder, 26 Rector St, died July 18; Miss Machett, Lumber & Rector, Newark, N. J., died Aug. 14.

	cholera	
1832	3,513	Deaths of cholera in city: *Annual Report from the City Inspector of the Interments . . . for the Year 1837* (1838): comparative statistics only. Reports of Cholera Cases, showing deaths, etc., in various city hospitals, 5 libers; Register of Cholera Patients admitted in the Park Hospital, showing deaths, dismissals, etc., 2 libers; Register of the N. Y. Rivington St. Hospital, 1 liber.[20]
1834	971	Deaths of cholera in city per above City Inspector's Report of 1837.
1849	5,161	Deaths of cholera per City Inspector's Report in Valentine's *Manual* for 1851; statistics only.

For almshouse records including deaths 1759–1847, see the Special Records section of this Guide, under Apprentices and the Poor.

PRINTED DEED INDEXES

Printed alphabetical indexes of the grantors and grantees of land in New York County, available in libraries, meet some of a searcher's needs in a minute's time. The period spanned by an individual's purchases and sales often gives a fairly good idea of that person's age. Other parties to the transactions are possible relatives, especially if of the same surname. In the grantor index the wife's first name is usually to be found. She may be a different person from the last spouse named in probate record or directory listing.

Index of Conveyances recorded in the office of Register of the city and county of New York: Grantees, 24 vols. in 9 (1858–64); Grantors, 26 vols. in 11 (1857–58); Grantors, Corporations (includes Masters in chancery and sheriffs) 1 vol. (1858).

An Essay towards an Improved Register of Deeds, City and County of New-York to Dec. 31, 1799 inclusive, Charles F. Grim, N. Y. 1832 (contains indexes of deeds on record in both N. Y. C. and Albany relating to N. Y. C. The wife is not so called in these indexes as she is listed alphabetically).

MARRIAGE NOTICES

The date by which a marriage has taken place may often be known through appearance of the wife in the grantor index of deeds, or through knowledge of the birthdate of a child. A general idea of the most likely marriage period may be deduced if the age at death of either party is known.

Even without a clue, a search should be made of the indexed marriage notices abstracted from newspapers (already listed in the Death Notices section). These notices are very important as they give the father of an unmarried bride. Also given is the officiating minister, although seldom his church or denomination.

---

[20] The cholera death records are among the records of the City Clerk's Office now in its storeroom in the Rhinelander Building. The City Clerk's Office is in the Municipal Building and its old records are in the charge of Mr. McLaughlin, Room 265. Many of the City Clerk's records are in process of being transferred to the Municipal Archives and Records Center at 238 William St., but the selection has not yet been made. See Stokes, VI:185–89 for description of records of the City Clerk's Office.

For marriage records, see the Special Records and the Church Records sections of this Guide.

MEANS OF IDENTIFYING THE CHURCH OF AN OFFICIATING MINISTER

Even though the officiating minister is given in the newspaper notice of marriage, it is often difficult to identify the church of that marriage; such identification is usually desired as a means of finding other church records of the family. Complete ministers' lists in handy form are available for the city's Dutch, Jewish, and Presbyterian churches. Many of the early directories and guides to the city have a list of ministers and/or a list of public buildings including churches but they are seldom complete; moreover, the ministers' names are more likely to be grouped by denomination than to be affixed to a particular church. Once the minister's denomination is known, it is feasible to consult the many printed histories of individual churches and the compilations of Greenleaf and Disosway. Since the early minister usually lived near his church, this church can often be identified if the searcher will patiently use contemporary city maps to relate some church (see church addresses in the Church Records section of this Guide) with the address listed for the minister in the main section of the city directory. Some ministers changed denomination as well as church, so identification must relate to the period of the marriage.

Manual of the Reformed Church in America 1628–1922, Charles E. Corwin, 5th ed., 1922.
Rise of the Jewish Community of New York, 1654–1860, Hyman B. Grinstein (Appx. v: List of Jewish Ministers).
The Presbyterian Church in New York City, Theodore Fiske Savage, 1949.
1805 *New-York Register and City Directory*, Longworth (lists churches with the minister of each in some instances; also sextons).
1827 *Description of the City of New-York*, James Hardie (lists 101 churches with the minister of each).
1837 *New-York as it is, in 1837*, pr. by J. Disturnell (lists 150 churches with the minister of each).
1850 Wilson's *The Great Metropolis or New-York Almanac for 1850*, pr. by Trow, at NYPL (has good list of churches, each with its address, minister and sexton).
History of the Churches . . . in the City of New York, Jonathan Greenleaf, 2nd ed., 1850.
The Earliest Churches of New York and Its Vicinity, Gabriel Disosway, 1865.
Annals of the American Pulpit, William B. Sprague, in 9 volumes, 1857–69.
Centennial History of the Protestant Episcopal Church in the Diocese of New York, 1785–1885, James G. Wilson, 1886.
Annals of New York Methodism, being a History of the Methodist Episcopal Church in the City of New York, Samuel A. Seaman, 1892.
Reminiscences of Baptist Churches and Baptist Leaders in New York City, 1835–1898, G. H. Hansell, 1899.

DIRECTORIES

The most important source for the searcher starting from "scratch" is the series of annual city directories, which commence in 1786. Starting with no more than a name, he can often "create" the family unit through patient study of these directories. My procedure has been to cull from the directories at intervals of 5 or

10 years the various appearances of the name, with a different column in my notes for each entry that looks like a different person — for instance, if I am interested in a John Jones, I may develop four columns (apart from scattered, seemingly unconnected appearances): one column for John Jones, porter or carter; one for John Jones, grocer, later merchant; one for John Jones, attorney, later judge, followed by "widow of John Jones" at the same address; one for John or John C. Jones, carpenter, builder, later real estate, followed several years after his disappearance by "Hannah Jones widow" at his last address or at an address in a similar locality. I then concentrate on the John Jones that seems most likely to be the one I am interested in, copying all individual and firm names under Jones that appear at his addresses: for his earlier directory years, these additional names will very likely be father and/or brothers, and maybe widowed mother; for his later directory years and afterward, these additional names will very likely be sons, through whose subsequent address perhaps their widowed mother may come to light. Family partnerships were prevalent in those days; changes in partnership name, address, and kind of business often lead to other possibilities, such as father-in-law, brothers-in-law, and sons-in-law.

A tentative unit, thus created, is sufficiently filled out as to both people and approximate life span to be provable through probate and death records, marriage and death notices, assuming that the family is not of so humble an economic and job status as not to appear in these sources.

For discussion of a special use for street directories, see the Census section of this Guide. Unfortunately there are only two street directories, for 1812 and 1851. The nearest equivalents, but for a limited city area, are: the 1789 rearrangement to be found in *The City of New York in . . . 1789*, Thomas E. V. Smith (1889), and Phillips' *Elite Carriage Directory* for 1874.

The very early city directories contain many small special lists that are of value in accumulating biographical items or leads, either to amplify knowledge of the individual concerned or to help in building the picture of, and thereby discarding, other persons of the same name. These directories are referred to below by publisher and date. The earliest directories were intended for selective business use (thus, only 1000 names are in the 1786 directory as compared with 5,742 white males aged 16 to 59 years in the 1786 statistical census). Specialized directories of various kinds were started in the mid-nineteenth century, the earliest being given below.

Roll of attornies, with the date admitted to practice before the courts (Hodge, Allen & Campbell's 1789 and 1790; Duncan's 1792 and 1795).

List of attornies resident in the country who have their agents in the city and the names of those agents, under Supreme Court rule of 1789 (Longworth's 1797).

Public notaries (Franks' 1786; Duncan's 1792; Langdon's 1804, etc.).

Members of the New-York Medical Society (Hodge, Allen & Campbell's 1789; Duncan's 1792–1794; Jones' 1805/6).

Officials and medical staff of the New-York Hospital, N.Y.C. Dispensary, N. Y. Public Dispensary, City Hospital at the Almshouse, Lying in Hospital (Duncan's 1792–1794; Longworth's 1799 and 1805; Elliot's 1812).

13

Sick nurses and midwives (Longworth's 1797; Groot & Elston's 1845).
Ministers of different denominations (in most of the 1780's and 1790's).
List of ecclesiastical establishments with their clergy (Longworth's 1805).
List of public buildings containing a good list of individual churches with their addresses (Longworth's 1803; Jones's 1805; Elliot & Crissy's 1811).
Churches in the city, their address, sexton, and burial grounds (Doggett's N. Y. C. & Co-Partnership Directory for 1843 and 1844).
Sextons who attend the different Burying Grounds in the city (Longworth's 1805).
Officers of the Society of Associated Teachers (Longworth's 1797 and 1799).
Teachers of the different charity schools (Longworth's 1805).
Columbia College, University of the State of New York, Free School Society of New York, Academy of Arts (Duncan's 1792; Longworth's 1799; Elliot's 1812).
Private male and female schools and seminaries (Driggs' Professional Directory for 1837/8).
Military officers of New York regiments (Hodge, Allen & Campbell's 1789; Duncan's 1792; Jones's 1805; etc.).
Members of the Society of the Cincinnati (Franks' 1786; Longworth's 1799; etc.).
Commissioners of forfeiture (Franks' 1786).
Officials of New York City including lists such as justices of the peace, inspectors, assessors, collectors, constables, marshals, commissioners of the almshouse (Hodge, Allen & Campbell's 1789; Duncan's 1792–1794; Jones' 1805/6).
Officers of the Port of New York including Collector of Customs and Health Officer, also pilots, inspectors, measurers, etc. (Franks' 1787; Hodge, Allen & Campbell's 1789; Duncan's 1792–1794; Longworth's 1799; Jones' 1805/6).
New York Mariners Friendly Society (Longworth's 1799).
Marine directory: list of packets and market boats, alphabetically by the towns they sail from (Longworth's 1803 and 1816/17).
Lists of engineers, firemen and fire companies, of foremen, and fire wardens (Duncan's 1792 and 1795; Longworth's 1796 and 1797; Elliot & Crissy's 1811; Langdon's 1804).
New York Chamber of Commerce (Duncan's 1792; Longworth's 1799).
Officers of The New-York Manufacturing Society (Hodge, Allen & Campbell's 1790; Duncan's 1792).
Directors and officers of the various banks and insurance companies (Longworth's 1796 and 1813, and most years).
Members of Gold & Silver Smith's Society, of General Society of Mechanics & Tradesmen, of the Society of Peruke-makers, Hairdressers, etc. (Franks' 1786 and 1787).
Franklin Typographical Ass'n. (Longworth's 1801 and 1802); Typographical Society (Elliot's 1812).
Society of House Carpenters, Society of Coopers, etc. (Low's 1796; Longworth's 1799); Company of Master Builders (Langdon's 1804).
Society of Cordwainers, Journeymen Saddlers Society, Society of Hatters, Mechanics Society (Longworth's 1801, 1810, 1811 and 1812).
N. Y. Agricultural Society (Duncan's 1792 and 1793; Longworth's 1799).
List of butchers and their stalls at the six markets (Longworth's 1802).
List of cartmen (i.e. carriers and truckers) by license number (Duncan's 1795; Low's 1796); Cartmen's Society, cartmen who are inspectors of hay, list of porters at the markets (Longworth's 1799 and 1801).
Proprietors of coaches (Hodge, Allen & Campbell's 1789).
New England Society, officials, counsellors and committee of (Elliot's 1812).
German Society, St. George's, St. Andrew's, St. Patricks, Thistle and Caledonian societies (Hodge, Allen & Campbell's 1789; Duncan's 1792; Longworth's 1799; Elliot's 1812).
French masonic lodges: L'Union Francaise, French Lodge la Sincerite (Longworth's 1805, 1810 and 1816/17).
Literary institutions: New York Society Library, Calliopean Society, Horanian Society (Longworth's 1796).
Musical societies: N. Y. Musical, Uranian, Harmonical, Columbian Anacreontic, St. Cecilia (Duncan's 1792–1794; Longworth's 1799).
Social: St. Stephens Society, Friary or Society of Black Friars (various years 1793–1799).

Benevolent institutions: Provident, Benevolent Society, Society for relief of distressed prisoners, Manumission Society, Magdalene Society, Society for the relief of poor widows with small children (Hodge, Allen & Campbell's 1789; Duncan's 1792; Longworth's 1799; Elliot's 1812).

Tammany Society: (in most years 1789–1799; Jones' 1805/6; Elliot's 1812).

Officials of the Grand Lodge and of various masonic lodges (Hodge, Allen & Campbell's 1789; and in many early years).

Deaths in New York City and County except Bloomingdale and Harlem, May 1814 to June 1816 (Longworth's 1815 and 1816/17).

List of streets with description (Longworth's 1799/1800, 1803–4, 1804; Jones's 1805–6; Elliot & Crissy's 1811).

Elliot's *Improved New-York Double Directory for 1812* (including directory by streets, containing occupant(s) of each building).

Doggett's New York City Street Directory for 1851 (directory by streets, containing occupant(s) of each building and the trade).

Brooklyn directory included with N. Y. C.'s (Low's 1796; Longworth's 1802 and 1811).[21]

Trade directory indexed by 105 trades (included in Longworth's city directory 1805).

New York Mercantile & General Directory for 1805–6, Jones (N. Y. C. residents listed within 10 occupational groups: learned professions and public officers, merchants, grocers, carpenters, masons, smiths, mechanics, shipmasters, cartmen, miscellaneous).

Classified Mercantile Directories for the cities of New-York and Brooklyn, pr. J. Disturnell, 1837 (individuals and firms classified into mercantile, professional and manufacturing groups; 3½ pp. 2-column index of trades and occupations).

New York City Professional Directory for 1837–8, Driggs (legal, medical, clergymen, dentists, private schools, literary and scientific institutions), at NYHS.

New York Business Directory for 1840 and 1841, Francis F. Ripley (8 pp. 2-column index of trades and occupations, e.g. 7 kinds of brokers, minute breakdown of drygoods and merchants).

New-York City and Co-Partnership Directory for 1843 and 1844, Doggett.

New York City Mercantile & Manufacturers' Business Directory, West, Lee & Bartlett, 1856, at NYPL.

Pictorial Directory of New York, Jones & Newman, 1848 (colored elevations of all buildings on the chief streets, with house numbering and names of occupants).

---

[21] Earliest Brooklyn directory printed separately was in 1822.

NAME LISTS AND BIOGRAPHICAL SKETCHES BY OCCUPATION

The biographical approach to research is very important for this period. Even if names, dates, and relationships are all that is desired, it is seldom that the genealogist can produce first-class proof of a family unit in this period by recourse directly and only to what are referred to as genealogical sources. This is fortunate, because life in the New York City of that era is fascinating and some facet of it should be reflected in any account of a family, no matter how humble. At that time the nation and New York were awakening and developing in almost any aspect one can think of. To mention only a few angles — As a royal province considered a source of raw materials supporting England's manufacturing and shipping, the many related industries and trades that might have competed had been restricted or prohibited in New York; with independence they grew apace, inventions and ingenuity supplying numerous sparks. In countless fields of endeavour, occupational and civic, are numerous "firsts" in the New York of that time. And its successful men were keenly alert to the problems of their surroundings; they engaged, in addition to at least one active business, in many civic activities which today are considered fulltime occupations, for example, savings banking (designed to help the poor) in which officers served without pay.

Early nineteenth century residents were frequently merchants, bankers, and volunteer firemen at some time in their career, hence the books of Scoville, Hardenbrook, and Costello are among the most useful guides to biographical clues, despite numerous inaccuracies. The widest range is covered by Bonner and by the occupational index to the Council Minutes.

If the problem in some aspect, whether business, social, civic, or church, leads to a long-established institution, look for an anniversary history — 75th, 100th, 150th, 200th; whether it be a serious study, a goodwill pamphlet, or a fund-raising aid, it may readily provide desired information or mention another side of a person's

16

life which on investigation may lead to what is wanted. The answers are seldom quickly forthcoming (with proof) in this period, but when found they are rich in many facets of the city's life. The following list is not intended to be inclusive but rather suggestive. Numerous related items and additional groups will be found in the accompanying sections of this Guide: Directories, Other Name Lists, and Secondary and Other Sources. In fact, the searcher should use these four sections as a unit. City and state officials will be found in the Special Records section and the military under Military Records, while ministers are covered in the section Means of Identifying the Church of a Minister.

COMPENDIUMS

New York, The World's Metropolis, 1623-4—1923-4, Wm. T. Bonner, 1924 (contains imposing number of biographical paragraphs grouped under: government administration, military history, welfare and professions, real estate and construction, wealth and finance, manufacturers and manufacturing, merchandise and merchandising, and transportation).

Minutes of the Common Council of the City of New York, 1784-1831 (1917-18), with master index in 2 vols. (The index analyzes 174 occupations; under the specific occupation, e.g. masons and bricklayers, are listed names of all persons so engaged who for some reason appear in the Minutes.)

Civil List & Constitutional History of the Colony and State of New York (1883 edition by Edgar A. Werner has good index of names).

The Burghers of New Amsterdam and The Freemen of New York 1675-1866, NYHS *Collections*, 1885 (occupation is usually given).

American Bibliography, with bibliographical and biographical notes, Charles Evans (11 vols. through 1797 pub. to date) (contains classified subject index, including subjects related to occupations; indexes of authors, printers and publishers).

Arts and Crafts in New York, 1777-1800, Rita S. Gottesman, to be published by NYHS (continuation of her earlier work; data from page by page survey of all N. Y. C. newspapers).

Hundred Year Book, being the Story of the Members of the Hundred Year Association of New York, Philip N. Schuyler, 1942 (110 business firms in the city over 100 years old).

Conspectus of American Biography, White, 2nd ed., 1937 (chronological lists, mostly U. S. officials; Americans preeminent in literature, the arts and sciences, and the professions, with date career began, pp. 306-57).

Dictionary of American Biography, Scribners (index vol., 1937, has index by occupations, pp. 360-474, but without dates).

FIREMEN

Our Firemen: A History of the New York Fire Departments, Volunteer and Paid. Augustine E. Costello, 1887.

Story of the Volunteer Fire Department of the City of New York, Geo. W. Sheldon, 1882.

Firemen's appointments 1804-1831: records in the City Clerk's Office as of 1927.[22]

BANKERS

Financial New York, Wm. T. E. Hardenbrook, 1897 (contains biographical sketches and portraits of very many early 19th century New Yorkers, not necessarily accurate but useful as suggestions; no index; a MS index at N. Y. Chamber of Commerce).

Over a Hundred Years Ago — And Today; The Bank for Savings (c.1928).

---

[22] Locations worded thus are intended to refer to the description as of 1927 of City Clerk's records in Stokes, VI:185-89, and to emphasize the uncertainty of location for a while, since many are soon to be transferred. See note 20 of this Guide.

A Century of Service, The Seamens Bank for Savings, 1829–1929.
History of the Bank of New York, 1784–1884, Hy. W. Domett.
The Merchants' National Bank of the City of New York, 1803–1903, Philip G.
   Hubert, Jr.
A Hundred Years of Merchant Banking: A History of Brown Brothers & Co.,
   Brown Shipley & Co., and the allied firms, John C. Brown, 1909.

MERCHANTS

The Old Merchants of New York City, Walter Barrett, 1863–66 [pseudonym of
   author Joseph A. Scoville], also later, larger editions (chatty and inaccurate
   but useful for suggestions).
"Supplement" by E. Cleave in *History of New York City,* Wm L. Stone, 1868
   (supplement covers the prominent mercantile houses, etc.).
History and Reminiscences of Lower Wall Street and Vicinity, Abram Wakeman,
   1914 (about the coffee and tea district and trades from colonial times).
"The Old Shipping Merchants of New York", G. W. Sheldon, in *Harpers Maga-
   zine* for 1892, 84:457–71.
Bonds of N. Y. C. auctioneers and auction sale accounts 1825–1839: 1 box at
   NYHS. See also papers at N. Y. County Clerk's Office, and Records of
   Commissions at NYSL.
One Hundred Years of Business Life, 1794–1894, W. H. Schieffelin & Co. (drug
   concern).
The House Flags of the Merchants of New York 1800–1860, F. Gray Griswold,
   1926.
*The Charter and By Laws with a History of the New York Chamber of Commerce
   . . . with notices of some of its most distinguished members,* 1849 (the history is an anniversary discourse by Charles King before the NYHS, 1848;
   volume contains list of members, 1844).
Chamber of Commerce of the State of New York, 65 Liberty St., New York,
   N. Y. (org. 1768): its library (est. 1832) is important for commerce, finance,
   and shipping; it has complete files of Hunt's Merchants' magazine 1839–
   1870 and of Foreign Commerce and Navigation (statistics) 1821 on.

SHIP CAPTAINS AND SHIPBUILDERS

*Square-Riggers on Schedule, The New York Sailing Packets to England, France,
   and the Cotton Ports,* Robert G. Albion, 1938. (Appx. XX: Biographical
   notes of packet captains.)
Rise of New York Port, 1815–1860, Robert G. Albion, 1939.
"The Old Shipbuilders" and "The Old Packet and Clipper Service", G. W.
   Sheldon, in *Harpers Magazine* for 1882 and 1884, 65:223–41 and 68:213–37.
"The Shipyard of America; History of Ship Building in New York; Names of
   Vessels Built, etc.," in *New York Herald* for Dec. 31, 1852, p. 6 (7-col. history from 1800).
Marine Society of the City of New York, instituted in the Year 1769, printed 1877
   and 1933 and at least eight other dates between 1781 and 1866 (lists of mem-
   bers from 1769 who are and who are not masters of vessels, with date of
   joining).

STOCK BROKERS

*Stocks and Stock-Jobbing in Wall-Street with Sketches of the Brokers and Fancy
   Stocks,* by a Reformed Stock Gambler, 1848 [Wm. Armstrong], at NYHS.

INSURANCE

The Knickerbocker Fire Insurance Company . . ., 1787–1875.
The Eagle Fire Co. of New York, 1806–1906, Louis N. Geldert.
Semi-Centennial History of the New-York Life Insurance Company, 1845–1895,
   James M. Hudnut.
The Insurance Blue Book, 1874, 1875, and Centennial Issue, 1877.
Insurance Society of New York, 107 William St., New York, N. Y.: its library
   (est. 1901) has material for the period of this Guide.

NATURAL HISTORY AND SCIENCES

History of the New York Academy of Sciences formerly the Lyceum of Natural History, Herman L. R. Fairchild, 1887 (org. 1817; book has 40 pp. of biographical accounts).

INDUSTRIES AND MANUFACTURING

Development of American Industries, John G. Glover & Wm. B. Cornell, 1941.
History of American Manufactures from 1608 to 1860, J. Leander Bishop in 3 vols., 3rd ed., 1868.
History of Manufacturing in New York City, 1825–1840, A.B. Gold, MS 1932 Master's thesis in Columbia University Library.
"New York (City) Iron Foundries", in *Morning Courier & New-York Enquirer* for May 1, 1852, p. 5.

SILVERSMITHS

American Silversmiths and their Marks, Stephen G. C. Ensko, 3rd ed., 1948.

ARTISTS AND DESIGNERS

Dictionary of Artists in America: about 10,000 Painters, Sculptors, Engravers, etc., who worked in the United States during the 300 years before the Civil War, George C. Groce, to be published by NYHS.
"New York Painting before 1800", George C. Groce, Jr., in *New York History* for 1938, 19:44–57.
History of the Rise and Progress of the Arts of Design in the United States, Wm. Dunlap, 1832 (chronological and biographical on painting, engraving, etc.)
Historical Annals of the National Academy of Design from 1825 to the Present Time, Thomas S. Cummings, 1865 (has only 6 pp. index but includes many deaths).
National Academy of Design Exhibition Record, 1826–1880, NYHS *Collections*, 1941–42 (includes year dates of birth and death or of activity).
The Century, 1847–1946 (history of The Century Association org. by artists and writers on art; lists members 1847–1946 with dates of membership and "D" if died when a member).
See also Booksellers below.

BOOKSELLERS, PRINTERS AND PUBLISHERS

Register of Artists, Engravers, Booksellers, Bookbinders, Printers and Publishers in New York City, 1633–1820, George L. McKay, 1942.
The Old Booksellers of New York and other Papers, Wm. L. Andrews, 1895.
"The Book Trade: Publishers and publishing in New-York", in *New York Daily Tribune*, issue of March 17, 1854 (sketches of various publishing houses).
American Bibliography, 1639–1820, Charles Evans (index of printers and publishers; see comment under Compendiums above).
Sketches of Printers and Printing in Colonial New York, Charles S. R. Hildeburn, 1895 (covers 33 persons active 1693–1807)
History and Bibliography of American Newspapers, 1690–1820, Clarence S. Brigham, 1947 (v. 2 has index of printers).

THE STAGE

History of the American Stage, containing Biographical Sketches of nearly every member of the profession that has appeared on the American stage, from 1733 to 1870, T. Allston Brown, 1870.
Annals of the New York Stage, George C. D. Odell, in 15 vols., 1927–48 (18th and 19th centuries to 1894; has many prints and photographs of actors and actresses).

MUSICIANS

The Philharmonic Society of New York, Henry E. Krehbiel, 1892 (includes officers and programs of the concerts 1842–1892).

INFORMATION OFFICE ON SERVANTS, ETC.

Licenses of intelligence offices 1817–1823 and 1847–1859: records in the City Clerk's Office as of 1927.[22]

TAVERN AND HOTEL KEEPERS

Old Taverns of New York, Wm. H. Bayles, 1915 (covers over 100 tavernkeepers 1643–1833).

Tavernkeepers' licenses, N. Y. C., 1784–1796 and 1808–1809: 2 vols. of records at NYHS.

Tavern licenses arranged by streets and alphabetically by proprietors' names, 1819 and 1826–1829; records now in the Municipal Archives and Records Center, 238 William St.

Card index of references to hotelmen of N. Y. C., W. Johnson Quinn, at NYHS.

MECHANICS AND TRADESMEN

Annals of the General Society of Mechanics and Tradesmen of the City of New York, from 1785 to 1880, eds. Thos. Earle & Chas. T. Congdon, 1882 (has list of members 1785–1881). See also *Charter and By-Laws* . . ., 1839 and 1856 (lists of members with election date and star if deceased).

Charter, By-Laws . . . *of the Mechanics' Institute of the City of New York,* 1854, at NYHS (org. before incorporation 1853, to develop special training; lists officials and life members with trade of each; lists members).

Licensed dealers in second-hand articles 1828–1859: records in the City Clerk's Office as of 1927.[22]

General Society of Mechanics and Tradesmen of the City of New York: its library (est. 1820) is at 20 West 44th St., New York, N. Y.

CARPENTERS

N. Y. Union Society of Journeyman House Carpenters' membership roll 1833–1836, at NYHS.

BUTCHERS

The Market Book, containing a historical account of the public markets in the cities of New York . . ., Thos. F. DeVoe, 1862 (he was superintendent of markets in N. Y. C.)

Notes on early Butchers and Markets in several volumes, Thos. F. DeVoe, at NYHS.

List of Butchers holding stalls in Fulton Market and in Catharine Market 1823–1832: records in the City Clerk's Office as of 1927.[22]

CARTMEN AND HACKDRIVERS

List, licenses and oaths of cartmen and porters, c1810 and 1816–1839: records now in the Municipal Archives and Records Center, 238 William St.

Licenses of hack owners and drivers 1817–1823 and 1840–1854: records in the City Clerk's Office as of 1927.[22]

List of New York City cartmen 1792–1797, at NYHS.

LAWYERS

The New York State constitution of 1777 says that all attorneys, solicitors, and counsellors at law hereafter to be appointed shall be appointed by the court and licensed by the first judge of the court in which they shall respectively plead or practice. According to the law of 1787, every person hereafter to be admitted as counsellor, attorney, solicitor, advocate, or proctor shall be examined by the judges or justices of the same court and such only as shall be found virtuous and of good fame and of sufficient learning and ability shall be admitted; their names shall be put in a roll to be kept in each court especially for that purpose; such as shall be found in default of record or otherwise shall be put out of the roll and never after be received to act as such in any court.

Citizenship was first required by 1806 rule of the Supreme Court for practice before its court, and the requirement of citizenship became law by the Revised Statutes of 1829. These Revised Statutes continued the system of appointing and licensing to practice by the courts in which the applicants intended to practice, and a proposal that attorneys licensed by the Supreme Court be permitted to practice in all courts was defeated.

According to the New York State constitution of 1846 and resultant 1847 law, every solicitor in Chancery and every attorney of the Supreme Court as of July 1, 1847 shall be entitled to practice in *all* courts of the state; every attorney of the Court of Common Pleas as of July 1, 1847 shall be entitled to practice in the county court of that county; and *every* applicant for admission to practice law shall apply to and be examined by the Justices of the Supreme Court, and on being found to be a male citizen 21 years of age, of good moral character, and of sufficient learning and ability, shall be entitled to practice in *all* courts of this state. Chester's history merely says that power of admission to the bar was vested in the Supreme Court until 1871, when by law it passed to the Court of Appeals.[28]

Roll of Attorneys 1754–1847, 1847–1895 in 2 libers at New York County Clerk's Office, Hall of Records, Chambers St., New York, N. Y. (admissions to practice before the Supreme Court and the Court of Chancery, arranged by first letter of surname, chronologically; after 1847 by the Supreme Court for all courts). Also signed parchment rolls 1754–1895.

Admissions to the Bar, papers relating to, 1799–1895, at *ibid*.

Legal Education in Colonial New York, Paul M. Hamlin, 1939 (has lists of N. Y. lawyers and barristers, in chronological groups 1664–1784; and members of the superior courts, arranged by ranks held, 1683–1783).

Attorneys of the Supreme Court in the Year 1789, compiled from the original rolls, in *Old New York*, ed. by Pasco, v. 1, Sept. 1889, pp. 126–30 (alphabetical list of about 150 lawyers, with dates admitted to practice from 1754).

Constitution of the Law Association of the City of New York, incorporated 1796, with the names of officers and members, 1837 (lists 200 members).

The Law Diary for 1859, pr. Hy. Anstice & Co., 1858, at NYHS (lists lawyers in N.Y.C. and Brooklyn, pp. 7–23, and notaries pp. 24–27).

Review of the Association of the Bar of the City of New York, together with Portraits and Autographs of Officers and Members brought down to the Year 1900, Frank Thompson, 1900 (has list of those who signed 1869 to organize the Ass'n, those deceased by 1900 being starred).

History of the Bench and Bar of New York, ed. by Hon. David McAdam, 1897, vol. 1 (pp. 244–524, biographical paragraphs on early men) and vol. 2.

History of the American Bar, Charles Warren, 1911 (pp. 292–304 on the Early State Bar of New York, referring to some publications on N.Y.C. lawyers active 1775–1825).

Pleasantries about Courts and Lawyers of the State of New York, Charles Edwards, 1867 (items on about 200 lawyers).

Tributes to Lawyers: Pamphlet *Addresses* and *Memorials* collected by Cephas Brainerd, in 25 vols., at N.Y.C. Bar Assn. Library.

Lives of Eminent Lawyers and Statesmen of the State of New York, Lucien B. Proctor, in 2 vols, 1882.

A Century and a Half at the New York Bar, Hy. Waters Taft, 1938 (concerns the law firm of Cadwalader, Wickersham and Taft).

Cravath Firm and its Predecessors, 1819–1947, Robert T. Swaine, 1946.

Association of the Bar of the City of New York, 42 West 44th St., New York, N. Y.: its library (est. 1870) has excellent collection of records and briefs.

---

[28] For 1777 and 1787 items, see *Laws of New York*, Greenleaf, 2nd ed., 1798, 1:11 & 356; *Courts and Lawyers of New York, A History 1609–1925*, Alden Chester, 1:887.

Other items in Laws of New York 1847, Chap. 280, §75 and *A Treatise on the Practice of the Supreme Court of the State of New York*, Claudius L. Monell, 2nd ed., v. 1 (1853), pp. 94-104.

A state law of 1792 (similar to a 1760 law) required for commencing practice in New York City examination and approval by any two of a specified list of state and city officials. A state law of 1806 authorized the incorporation of medical societies and empowered them to examine medical students and confer diplomas constituting a license to practise physic or surgery or both in the state; hereafter no one could commence practice until he received such diploma from one of the medical societies to be established. The county medical societies held the power to license practitioners in medicine, 1806–1880. But they had exclusive control for only three years, as under a law of 1809 graduates of medical schools in the state, granted a degree by the Regents, were entitled to practise without examination.[24] The present Medical Society of the County of New York, organized 1806 (as successor of an earlier medical society in the city), informs me that it has neither lists of those whom it licensed under the above law nor a list of members during its first half-century. The catalogues of college alumni in the next section will be helpful, as also the listings in the Directories section of this Guide.

Account of Bellevue Hospital with a Catalogue of the Medical and Surgical Staff from 1736 to 1894, Robert J. Carlisle, 1893 (catalogue of the staff is 220 pp.).

Charter of the Society of the New York Hospital and the Laws Relating Thereto, 1856 (lists Governors 1770–1856 with dates of service; lists physicians and surgeons 1770–1856 with dates of service and of death).

The Medical Register of the City of New York and vicinity to which is also added, Contributions to the Medical History of the City of New York, printed often from 1862 on (title varies) (includes many early lists of doctors and other material within the scope of this Guide).

Physicians in the city in 1786, 1793, and 1798: culled from the city directories and printed in the above *Register* for 1862, pp. 157–58 and 163–64.

Chronological list, with biographical notes, of 437 Physicians who have been members of The New-York Historical Society 1804–1947, MS at NYHS.

Notes for a Civil List of the Province of New York: O'Callaghan Papers, Box III, at NYHS. (His working notes on doctors give for each through 1776 a year date, the county, and an occasional biographical note and death date; not referenced but include doctors known to have been in N.Y.C. after the Revolution.)

Reminiscences of Medical Teaching and Teachers in New York, Valentine Mott, 1850.

American Medical Biography, James Thacher, 1828.

American Medical Biography, Stephen W. Williams, 1845.

American Medical Biography, S. D. Gross, 1861.

Distinguished Living New York Surgeons, Samuel W. Francis, 1866.

Distinguished Living New York Physicians, Samuel W. Francis, 1867.

Portraits of the Noted Physicians of New York, 1750–1900, with a few facts in the life of each, Walter G. Eliot, 1900.

New York Academy of Medicine, 2 East 103rd St., New York, N. Y.: its library (est. 1847) is so excellent that the New York Public Library refers people to it and stocks little on medical biographies and history.

---

[24] *History of Medicine in New York*, James Joseph Walsh, 1919, pp. 73–85. No early licenses for doctors have turned up as a result of my inquiries to: N. Y. State Library, State Medical Library, New York County Clerk's Office, and Medical Society of the County of New York.

An occasional medical diploma from out of town is registered in the liber Index of Misc. Papers No. 2 (c1812–c1891) at the N. Y. County Clerk's Office.

The membership list is a most suggestive source for biographical leads and sometimes for clues to the life span of an individual. Many such lists are printed; others may be obtained or examined. They usually give the year-date of joining and sometimes the year-date of decease, or an asterisk indicating decease which is useful if one procures an early list. Early nineteenth century New Yorkers were habitually active in many and varied civic services and interests, so their names are to be found on many membership lists such as the Society of The New York Hospital and the Free School Society, the early Philharmonic Society and the New York Society Library, societies of origin such as the New England and St. Andrew's, benevolent institutions such as Tammany then was, and masonic and church or kindred organizations such as the American Bible Society.

Educational lists have a use similar to membership lists. The universities have done considerable research on their early graduates, and their alumni lists include condensed biographical data.

An effort has been made to keep related subjects together, although this may mean grouping people out of their field because of the tendency to varied civic services and interests. Thus, education, educational activities (civic), and literary life (including authors) are in this section, but hospitals (although their boards had many laymen) are grouped with doctors in the section Occupations. The benevolent societies connected with a gainful occupation are in that section or in the specialized lists in the Directories section of this Guide. The benevolent societies that today we would call charities are discussed in the descriptive guides to the city listed in my Secondary Sources section.

Since societies of origin usually denote an origin elsewhere, they are discussed in The Non-Native New Yorker section.

It is hoped that the following list is full enough to stimulate ideas of possible means for meeting the particular problem. If not, perhaps the telephone book will locate for the searcher an old organization still in existence.

EDUCATION AND TEACHING

Columbia University Officers and Alumni 1754–1857, Milton Halsey Thomas, 1936 (includes College of Physicians and Surgeons 1807–1857).

General Alumni Catalogue of New York University, 1916 (alumni, classes of 1833–1915, including the Medical Dep't formed 1838).

Register of the Associate Alumni of the College of the City of New York, c1916 (alumni 1853–1916).

Catalogue of the Faculty and Students of Rutgers Medical College, session 1826–27 (1827).

Private boarding and day schools, 2 columns of advertisements by, in *New-York Daily Tribune* for Aug. 31, 1852.

Proceedings of the Thirteenth Annual Commencement and Circular of Rutgers Female Institute, 1852, at NYHS (lists students from infants up, honor students, teachers, graduates of classes 1840–52, home addresses of students and graduates).

Manual of the Board of Education of the City and County of New-York, printed 1847 and thereafter (lists commissioners, committeemen, inspectors and

trustees of common schools, etc.; lists ward schools, public schools and
special schools, with addresses and teachers of each, pp. 26–76).

*History of the Collegiate Reformed Dutch Church in the City of New York, from
1633 to 1883,* Henry W. Dunshee, 1853 and 1883 (includes list of students
1791–1883, with age, father, and home address).

Account of the Free School Society of New York, 1814 (has trustees 1805 and 1814,
donors and subscribers).

History of the Public School Society of the City of New York, Wm. O. Bourne,
1870 (the records of this society 1807–1853 are at NYHS).

LITERARY LIFE

History of the New York Society Library, Austin B. Keep, 1908 (founded 1754).

*Lecture on the past, the present, and the future of the New-York Society Library
. . . 1856,* John MacMullen, 1856 (lists trustees and persons holding rights
1856, pp. 29–42).

"Early Literary Clubs in New York City", Eleanor B. Scott, in *American Literature* for 1933, 5:3–16.

*Revised Constitution and By-Laws of the Columbian Peithologian Society, with a
List of Members from (its) Foundation . . . 1806,* N. Y. 1849, at NYHS
(for oratory and debate).

*Charter, Laws . . . of the Literary and Philosophical Society of New-York; with
a List of the Officers and Members,* 1818, at NYHS (gives member's occupation).

Constitution and By-Laws of The New-York Athenaeum, 1825, at NYHS (org.
1824 for the cultivation of science, literature and the arts; lists members).

Third Annual Report of The New-York Lyceum, instituted 1838 (1842), at NYHS
(lists members).

*Address to the People of the United States in behalf of the American Copyright
Club,* N. Y. 1843, at NYHS (lists members of this club with addresses).

New York in Literature; the Story told in the Landmarks of Town and Country,
Rufus R. Wilson, 1947.

The New York of the Novelists, Arthur B. Maurice, 1917.

Literary New York, the Landmarks and Associations, Charles Hemstreet, 1903.

American Bibliography, 1639–1820, Charles Evans (has index of authors; see
my comment in the Occupational section under compendiums).

MASONIC LODGES

The New Free-Mason's Monitor; or, Masonic Guide, James Hardie, 1818 (has list
of lodges in New York State, with no., title, place of meeting and date of
warrant).

*History of the most ancient and honorable fraternity of free and accepted Masons in
New York from the earliest date,* Charles T. McClenachan, 1888 (lists members 1784–1789 of St. John's Independent Royal Arch Lodge No. 2 and
members 1784–1785 of St. John's Lodge No. 1, org. 1757, N. Y. C.).

Holland Lodge . . . of Free and Accepted Masons: Membership, By Laws . . .,
1930 (org. 1787 in N. Y. C.; includes necrology from 1787 with date of admission, and masters and wardens with year of election).

Headquarters: Grand Secretary, Masonic Hall, 71 West 23rd St., New York, N. Y.

VARIED MEMBERSHIPS

Tammany Society's membership roll 1789–1916: photostat at NYPL.

*Tammaniana, Society of Tammany or Columbian Order in the City of New
York,* MS by Edwin P. Kilroe, at NYHS (members 1789–1924, alphabetical
and chronological; officers 1789–1924, by years and classified).

Charter . . . of the American Agricultural Association, adopted 1846 (1846), at
NYHS (lists members).

*Charter and By-Laws of the Society for the Promotion of Useful Arts . . . with a
list of the Members,* 1815, at NYHS (org. 1804; gives standing committees
on agriculture, chemistry, mechanic arts, and fine arts).

*Plan of the Society for the Promotion of Industry, with . . . the Names of Sub-
scribers,* N. Y. 1816, at NYHS (organization of N.Y.C. women for the poor).

Society for the Encouragement of Faithful Domestic Servants in New-York, Annual
Reports 1826–1830, at NYHS (lists of subscribers and nurses).

Members of the New-York Historical Society, Feb. 1845 (with asterisks against names of deceased); MS register of members 1804–1901 at NYHS.
Mother of Clubs, Being the History of the First Hundred Years of the Union Club of the City of New York 1836–1936, Reginald T. Townsend.
U. S. Military Philosophical Society membership 1789–1813, at NYHS.

WEALTH

Wealth, actual and comparative, is an interesting angle that can seldom be pursued without much time spent in research. However, there are a few printed tax lists and chatty credit guides, the latter being especially useful as a clue to how the wealth was obtained. One should not overlook estate figures in the later probate records and prices in records of property sales. For comparative wealth, lists of voters and jurors may be useful depending on the date, so the searcher might do well to inquire into the qualifications for the period he is interested in. Thus for the period 1777–1821, under the first state constitution, residents in order to qualify as voters (electors) for the Assembly had to have a specified minimum value of property owned or rented — for some discussion of this aspect in connection with the electoral censuses, see the Census Records section of this Guide.

1791 Assessment of real and personal property in the East Ward, NYHS *Collections*, 1911.
1793, 1795, 1796 tax lists: 3 official volumes now at NYHS.
1795 (about) List of principal private residences and their value; List of principal wealthy citizens: in Valentine's *Manual*, 1855, pp. 561, 565.
1815 and 1820 Those taxed on over $5000 personal property, names and figures from the tax lists: in Valentine's *Manual*, 1864, p. 755.
1829 and 1830 Assessment books now at NYHS.
1850 *List of Persons, Copartnerships & Corporations, who were taxed on $17,500 and Upwards in the City of New York in the Year 1850*, Wm. A. Darling, deputy receiver of taxes, at NYPL (gives name, tax on personal estate, tax on real estate, total valuation).
Wealth and Biography of the Wealthy Citizens of New York City, Moses Y. Beach, in 13 edns. 1842–1855, of which 6th ed., 1845, is reprinted in *Century of Banking in New York*, H. W. Lanier, 1922. (These are the earliest credit guides, listing fortunes estimated at over $100,000; the biographical comments, by Beach, editor of the N. Y. Sun, are not reliable and are sometimes derogatory, but are useful for leads especially on how the fortune was made.)
Aristocracy of New York: Who They Are and What They Were; being a Social and Business History of the City for many Years, 1848 [Wm. Armstrong] at NYPL (similar to the preceding item).
Reuben Vose's Wealth of the World Displayed, R. Vose, 1859, at NYPL (chatty, about rich New York City people).
1790 etc. Tax Book of East, South, North and West Wards and of Harlem Division.
c1789–1848 Tax Books by Wards, over 700 libers.
1824–1831 Assessment Book of 1st to 14th Wards and of 16th Ward, North Section.
1843–1854 Personal Taxes (these last four groups of records are in the city's possession).[25]

---

[25] Tax books and the 1821 electoral census are among the many records now under the jurisdiction of the Comptroller's Office which in 1927 (see Stokes, VI:194–202) were under the Dep't of Finance. They are now stacked without order and mostly without labels in a dark basement of the Municipal Building. They are both inaccessible and difficult to identify. It would be advisable for searchers to contact Mr. Buchholtz, the Chief Clerk, Room 520, Municipal Building, Chambers St., New York, N. Y., well in advance, with a reason for the search, so they will go to the trouble of locating desired volumes and carting them across the street to a public search room.

Various name lists may be used for one purpose or another, especially when conveniently at hand.

1808 Names of Persons who voted in the 3rd Ward, April 1808, being electors for the Assembly 1809, at NYHS (4 vols., one is more inclusive being the names of residents in the 3rd ward with addresses, listing whether Federal, Democrat or doubtful, and having occasional remarks: removed, dead, alien, absent) (see above comment under Wealth).

1825 *List of jurors in New York City taken 1825* (1827) at NYHS (alphabetical list of names by wards, with address and occupation).

State and Federal census records, which contain much statistical data.

Printed alphabetical indexes of grantees and grantors of land, available in libraries.

Typed alphabetical indexes of testators and of intestate estates, available in libraries.

For the 3 preceding entries, see also the sections: State and federal censuses, Printed deed indexes, and Probate and related records.

Printed alphabetical indexes of defendants and complainants in equity suits, 1823–1855, at NYPL (see also Special Records Section, under Courts).

SECONDARY AND OTHER SOURCES

If there is reason to believe that the desired family or an individual in it was prominent, it is worthwhile looking in the various biographical encyclopedias such as the American, Scribner, National, and Appleton, in the few publications dealing with a restricted number of local families such as Hamm, Pelletreau, Reynolds, and Cutler, and in various histories of the city, especially Stokes and Bonner.

Of inestimable value for the initial survey will be a card index being prepared by Gunther E. Pohl (of the Genealogy Division of the NYPL). It is a biographical and portrait index to histories of New York State and its subdivisions, including local biographical compendiums, about 100,000 references arranged alphabetically with birth-date to facilitate identification.

As a rule, this period requires original research. Helpful are: guides to records and depositories; guides to and accounts of the city, its local sections, and its institutions; diaries and reminiscences; publications on and by special population groups; and lists of portraits — to give perhaps the most important categories. Of the many accounts, more or less accurate, of local areas such as Maiden Lane and Stuyvesant Village, very few are listed here as a good (but not complete) list is to be found in Stokes, VI:252–54. Publications of the U. S. Catholic, the American Irish, and the American Jewish Historical Societies are obvious possibilities for some work.[26] The particular problem should give rise to the query whether there is an account of the particular local area, institution, or population group. The following list is not intended to be complete: it includes the most generally helpful sources and suggests some little-used sources as possibilities.

---

[26]For further data on special population groups, see the section Origin Outside of New York City, which follows

GUIDES TO RECORDS AND DEPOSITORIES

The Iconography of Manhattan Island, 1498–1909, I. N. Phelps Stokes, in 6 vols. (see comment in Special Records section of this Guide).

"Report on the Public Archives of New York", H. L. Osgood, in American Historical Association, *Annual Report* for 1900, 2:67–250 (covers archives of Greater N. Y. C. and of New York State; still an important guide despite 1911 Fire losses).

Guide to the Principal Sources for Early American History (1600–1800) in the City of New York, Evarts B. Greene & Richard B. Morris, 1929 (addenda in preparation).

Guide to Vital Statistics in the City of New York: Borough of Manhattan —Churches, W.P.A., 1942.

Inventory of the Church Archives in New York City, W.P.A. (volumes by denominations: only some covered).

Survey of The Manuscript Collections in The New-York Historical Society, 1941.

Catalogue of American Genealogies in the Library of the Long Island Historical Society, 1935 (has an unusually good collection of little known and privately printed genealogies).

New York Public Library, *Bulletin,* vol. 5 (1901) has check lists on various subjects relating to N. Y. C., including maps, schools, clubs, charities, etc.

Directory Information Material (Printed) for New York City Residents, 1626–1786, John H. Moriarty, 1942 (covers sources on life in N. Y. C. from viewpoint of name lists, indicating period covered, which is often into the 19th century).

Laws of the State of New York relating particularly to the City of New York, Hy. E. Davies, 1855 (NYPL call No. *SY) (covers period 1691–1855).

Special Libraries Directory of Greater New York, 1950 (brief description of collections).

Guide to Manuscript Depositories in New York City, W.P.A., 1941 (covers 68 institutions; badly arranged for easy use, but useful for the smaller collections).

Guide to Depositories of Manuscript Collections in New York State (exclusive of New York City), v. 1, W.P.A., 1941; Supplement, 1944.

Historical Societies in the United States and Canada: A Handbook, American Association for State and Local History, 1944 (has brief description of their libraries).

ACCOUNTS OF THE CITY, ITS LOCAL SECTIONS, AND INSTITUTIONS

The City of New York in the year of Washington's Inauguration 1789, Thomas E. V. Smith, 1889.

Description of the City of New-York, James Hardie, 1827.

The Picture of New-York, and Stranger's Guide, A. T. Goodrich, 1828.

Williams' New York as it is, in 1833, pr. by Disturnell, 1833.

New York as it is, in 1837, pr. by Disturnell, 1837.

New-York, Past, Present and Future, E. Porter Belden, 1849.

History of the City of New York, Mary Louise Booth, 1 vol., 1867: extra illustrated copy in 8 vol. MS by Thomas A. Emmet, 1876, at NYPL.

Manuals of the Corporation of the City of New York, annually 1841/2–1866 ed. David T. Valentine, 1868–1870 ed. Shannon and Hardy, and New Series 1916/17–1927 ed. Hy. C. Brown; all known as *Valentine's Manuals.* Historical Index for the vols. 1841–1870 by Hufeland, 1900. Index to the illustrations in vols. 1841–1870, Society of Iconophiles, 1906. (Official manuals of the city supplemented by historical articles, extracts from records and newspapers, portraits, maps, etc. Supplementary material has inaccurate texts and unsound deductions but is valuable for suggestions.)
Index to Personal Names in the Historical Portions of Valentine's Manuals 1841–1866, Louis D. Scisco, 1948, MS at NYGB, 512 pp.

Old New York, in 2 vols., 1889–1891, ed. W. W. Pasko.

The New York of Yesterday: A Descriptive Narrative of old Bloomingdale, Hopper Striker Mott, 1908 (local history of the west side of Manhattan).

Harlem: its Origin and Early Annals . . . also Sketches of Numerous Families,
James Riker, 1881, enlarged and ed. by Toler & Potter, 1904 (its genealogies
go down to 1902).
Tour around New York and My Summer Acre, John Flavel Mines, 1893 (chatty
reminiscences on New York and New Yorkers in form of a city tour, especially of the country houses along the East River).
New York in Slices, by an Experienced Carver, 1849 [George G. Foster], at NYHS
(cynically chatty on various occupations and aspects of N.Y.C. life).

DIARIES AND LETTERS

1783–1806   *Correspondence and Journals of Samuel Blachley Webb,* v. III, 1894
(New England merchant in New York; Colonel in the Revolution).
1793–1799   Diary of Dr. Alexander Anderson, physician and engraver, in 3 vols.:
original MS at Columbia University, MS copy at NYHS, portion printed in
Pasko's *Old New York.*
1794–1798   Diary of life in New York City by John Anderson, Jr., lawyer: MS
at NYHS.
1797–1834   Diary of William Dunlap, artist, dramatist and historian, in NYHS
Collections, 1928–31.
1799–1806   Diary of Elizabeth De Hart Bleecker, kept in New York City:
original at NYPL.
1816–1833   Letters from John Pintard to his Daughter, in NYHS *Collections,*
1937–40.
1828–1851   *Diary of Philip Hone:* original in 28 vols. at NYHS, only about one-
quarter covered by the editions of Tuckerman, 1889, and of Nevins, 1927.
1835–1875   *Diary of George Templeton Strong,* 1952 (lawyer, on life in N. Y. C.).

REMINISCENCES

Reminiscences of an old New Yorker, Wm. A. Duer, 1867 (President of Columbia
College): extra illustrated copy, MS at NYPL.
Old New York: or, Reminiscences of the Past Sixty Years, John W. Francis, M.D.,
1 vol., 1858 and 1865: extra illustrated copies — 5 vol. MS by Thomas A.
Emmet, 1880, at NYPL; 13 vol. MS by Joseph F. Sabin from coll'n of Ogden
Goelet, 1896, at NYHS.
*Sketches and Impressions, Musical, Theatrical and Social, 1799–1885, from the after
dinner talk of Thomas Goodwin, Music Librarian,* R. Osgood Mason, 1887.
Reminiscences of an Octogenarian of the City of New York (1816 to 1860), Chas. H.
Haswell, 1896 (marine engineer).
Autobiography, with Personal Reminiscences of New York City from 1798 to 1875,
Nathaniel T. Hubbard, 1875 (by an old New York merchant in his 90th
year).
Memoirs and Letters of James Kent, Late Chancellor of the State of New York, by
his Great-Grandson, Wm. Kent, 1898 (lawyer and chancellor).
Recollections of a Resident of New York City from 1835 to 1905, John J. Sturte-
vant, MS copy at NYPL.
Fifty Years' Reminiscences of New-York, Grant Thorburn, 1845 (seedsman and
author).
Last Days of Knickerbocker Life in New York, Abram C. Dayton, 1882 (social
life about 1840).

GUIDES TO PORTRAITS

*Catalogue of American Portraits in The New-York Historical Society: Oil Portraits,
Miniatures, Sculptures,* 1941.
*Portrait Gallery of the Chamber of Commerce of the State of New York — Catalog
and Biographical Sketches,* George Wilson, 1890 (longer biographies than in
the 1924 ed.).
*A.L.A. Portrait Index: Index to Portraits contained in Printed Books and Periodi-
cals,* eds. Wm. C. Lane and Nina E. Browne, 1906.
Frick Art Reference Library, 10 East 71st St., New York, N. Y.: has wonderful
photograph collection of portraits still privately owned, but the biographical
notes in its files are unreliable.

THE NON-NATIVE NEW YORKER

The sizable proportion of early New York City residents who came from elsewhere in the state or the United States or from abroad is shown by their birthplaces given on the city's death records — see my table of birthplaces compiled from Death Register No. 1 (1801–1814), in the Death Records section of this Guide.

An excellent study is Robert Ernst's *Immigrant Life in New York City 1825–1863* (1949). It has an outstanding bibliography; its tables include classification of occupations in the 1855 census — by country of foreign birth and by relative status of the first and second generations.

The fact of naturalization and a possible clue (through length of residence) for dates of arrival and of naturalization are to be found in the 1855 census and in later death records, as already mentioned in those sections of this Guide.

ORIGIN OUTSIDE OF NEW YORK CITY

The origin of a New York City resident often constitutes a problem. Generally, the only source that is likely to supply the town of birth is the death record (marriage records being almost non-existent before 1853); the county of birth is given in the 1855 state census and the state of birth in the federal censuses; military pension papers may give the birthplace, or a clue to it if the regiment of service belonged to another state (many New York County residents listed on the federal 1835 pension roll had served from other states). I am under the impression that for the foreign-born the country of birth or allegiance is all that is usually given on various early records: census, passenger list, and naturalization. There is still another source for investigation: societies whose membership is limited to a particular origin. While this origin does not necessarily denote birthplace, membership rolls in such societies can be very helpful, and many are printed. For instance, if our man is an early member of the New England Society of New York City, the searcher — rather than look for him in the many New York City churches — might do well to concentrate on the records mentioned in this paragraph for leads back to a specific part of New England. Presence on a membership roll also indicates the possibility that the particular society may have biographical data (if only date of death) in its files or publications; or this may be the case in the records of some other society, church, or institution in which many of those active have the same origin: for example, St. Patrick's Society, St. Peter's Catholic Church, and the American Irish Historical Society might all have data on a particular individual.

Biographical Register of Saint Andrew's Society of the State of New York, 1756–1856, Wm. MacBean, in 2 vols. 1922–25 (comprehensive and well done for a large membership) (MacBean's notes, containing additional material, are at NYHS).

History of St. George's Society of New York, from 1770 to 1913 (lists members 1786–1913 and has biographies of officers).

Society of the Friendly Sons of St. Patrick: its Charter, constitution, by-laws, committees, roll of members, etc., 1909 (lists members 1784 on, after 1835 by election date; has photographs of its ex-presidents).

St. Patrick's Day: Its Celebration in New York . . . 1737–1845, John D. Crimmins, 1902 (has 550 biographical sketches).

In old New York, Michael J. O'Brien, 1928 (contains "Irish" names on tombstone inscriptions in Trinity and St. Paul's churchyards, Trinity Church records, wills, executors and witnesses, letters of administration, grantees and grantors in New York County records 1668–1800. These long lists may be useful for some other purpose than origin; they are more comprehensive than the Irish population could have been since the Catholic religion was prohibited in provincial New York).

Deutsche Gesellschaft der Stadt New York: its Charter and by-laws of the German Society of New York with a list of the members, 1808, at NYPL (lists members 1784–1808).

The German Society of the City of New York: Annual Report, January 1885 (lists those who have been members for at least 25 years, by year from 1839).

"The New England Society in the City of New York", Winthrop Packard, in *New England Magazine* for 1908, 37:523–47 (early history, with photographs of officials).

Report, Constitution and By-Laws of The New England Society in the City of New York, 1843 (org. 1805; lists members, starring those deceased).

Fifty-Fourth Annual Report of The New England Society in the City of New-York, 1859 (lists living members with dates of election).

Saint Nicholas Society of the City of New York: Genealogical Record, vols. I to IV, 1905–1934 (org. 1835, limited to descent from residents of New York State prior to 1785) (volumes contain lists of former officers with dates of service, lists of former members with dates of election; biographical sketches, not always accurate, of the New York ancestor, with references; ancestral line of each member with dates).

Rise of the Jewish Community of New York, 1654–1860, Hyman B. Grinstein, 1945 (excellent study; Appx. II is list of N. Y. C. synagogues before 1860, with date, locations, and racial origin of worshippers).

Portraits Etched in Stone: Early Jewish Settlers, 1682–1831, David de Sola Pool, 1952 (has 179 biographies of those buried in the New Bowery cemetery).

French Refugee Life in the United States, 1790–1800, Frances S. Childs, 1940 (few names, but excellent for background and bibliography).

List of 140 Frenchmen for whom letters are at the Post Office in New York City: in Aug. 21, 1795 issue of *Gazette Francaise et Americaine* (newspaper printed in N.Y.C. 3 days a week; file at NYHS).

"French Travellers in the United States 1765–1931: A Bibliographical List", Frank Monaghan, in NYPL *Bulletin* for 1932, v. 36 (cf list of travellers in N.Y.C., in Stokes' *Iconography*, VI:635–37).

Directory francais et Guide des affaires . . . Residents francais a New-York et aux environs . . ., Augustin P. Maugé, N. Y. 1864, at NYPL.

Catholic Footsteps in Old New York . . . from 1524 [sic] to 1808, Wm. H. Bennett, 1909 (chatty, but many names).

"Italians in New York during the first half of the Nineteenth Century", Howard R. Marraro, in *New York History* for 1945, 26:278–306.

St. David's Society of the State of New York (org. 1835 by Welsh Americans; predecessor society of 1801): pamphlet, 1947, giving ex-presidents and important members.

PASSENGER LISTS

Very few records have been preserved of passenger arrivals for the Federal period prior to 1820. The U. S. act of 1798 required that for two years all aliens coming into this country be recorded by the customs officials and reported to the Department of State. The U. S. act of 1799 required the listing on the vessel's manifest of all passengers, alien or native, cabin or steerage, who brought in baggage. Small groups of passengers (maybe 1 to 10 a ship) recorded under these two early laws have been found on the manifests of the customs records for various ports;[27] how many for New York awaits exhaustive study, but these manifests may list only a fraction of the immigrants to the Port of New York. Names of a few immigrants may be obtained from indentures (see Special Records section of this Guide under Apprentices and the Poor). From Lancour's excellent bibliography "Passenger Lists of Ships coming to North America, 1607–1825" (NYPL *Bulletin*, 41:389), I cull the few within the scope of this Guide:

for all American ports		where published
1800	Emigrant liverymen of London	NEHG, v. 60
1805–06	Passenger lists to America from Ireland	NEHG, v. 60, 61, 62, 66
1811	Passenger lists printed in Ireland 1811	Am. Irish Hist. Soc., v. 28
1815–16	Passenger lists printed in Ireland 1815–16	Am. Irish Hist. Soc., v. 29

for the port of New York		
1803–06	Early Irish emigrants (add'l to the above)	The Recorder, Boston, v. 3
1825	The Norse Mayflower	R. B. Anderson's The first Chapter of Norwegian Immigration 1821–1840

[27] Article by Meredith B. Colket, Jr., in NEHG *Register* 106:203, which also states that examination of Dep't of State records for the period has failed to reveal reports mentioned in this act of 1798.

To facilitate an exhaustive search for records of passenger arrivals 1798–1819 at the Port of New York, the following summarizes my information, gathered in compiling this Guide: —
Descriptions of records at the N. Y. Custom House as of 1929 and 1938–39 are to be found in Greene & Morris' Guide, p. 264 and in Robert G. Albion's studies of the port and of sailing packets under bibliography. The latter says, without giving dates: "Cargo manifests are not available for this early period, having been destroyed by fire"; "(records) . . . reveal little about their cargoes, since manifests are preserved for only ten years"; "the passenger lists are not open to general inspection, but information of particular vessels from 1819 on may be had upon request to the Records Division. The state records of immigration have been destroyed by fire."
Mr. F. B. Laughlin, Asst. Collector, Bureau of Customs, New York, wrote me Aug. 29, 1952 that the New York office has no manifests or passenger lists for the period 1798–1819 (that I inquired about), that their lists do not indicate whether any such might have been included in the records sent April 1943 to the National Archives, Washington, at which time were sent all historical records for the years 1789 to 1900 then in existence in the N. Y. Custom House.
In the National Archives collections are names of some passengers for this 1798–1819 period. Mr. Meredith B. Colket, Jr., of the General Reference Section, National Archives, Washington, D. C., wrote me Sept. 3, 1952: It is my understanding that the National Archives did not receive any manifests for this period from the Collector of Customs at New York City. It did receive some from the Library of Congress which had previously acquired them. These manifests appear to be interfiled with correspondence and their degree of completeness is unknown. They appear to consist of incoming manifests (foreign), outgoing manifests (foreign), incoming manifests (coastwise), and outgoing manifests (coastwise). Among the incoming manifests (foreign) are occasional baggage lists which give the names of incoming passengers. They are a potential source of material of genealogical interest but, because of their arrangement, very difficult to use for genealogical purposes until they are indexed.
At Sag Harbor, Long Island, in charge of the Old Sagg-Harbour Committee, are some historical records of this period, including a ship register, enrolment ctf. and clearance papers of 3 different ships and the 1809–1815 record book of the Sag Harbor Collector of Customs (per the above Mr. Laughlin). I made no Sag Harbor inquiries.
At NYHS are a few N. Y. Custom House papers: Oaths of entry 1790–1799, papers of various ships 1800–1835, and the 1804 papers of one ship, in 6 boxes. Casual inspection of occasional papers picked at random disappointed me in their paucity of names; while I did see lists of boxes and cargo, sometimes with a person's name appended against each item, these names were not explained and might have been consignees. I saw no indication of passengers but I made no thorough examination.
At NYSL had been deposited colonial records of the N. Y. Custom House. They are still there to the extent that they survived the 1911 Fire. Miss Edna L. Jacobsen, Associate Librarian, wrote me Aug. 26, 1952 confirming my understanding that manifests at NYSL cover only the colonial period.
At the Dep't of Welfare, N. Y. C., as of 1927 (see Stokes, VI:210) are: bond register of ships 1818–1841 in 4 libers; also in a liber of boys and girls bound 1794–1815, on p. 220, begins a ships' list with names of captains, bond sureties, etc., 1818–19. The location of these records is suggestive of the possibility that they might concern indentured immigrant passengers.

In the British Museum, London, are 267 ships' manifests containing American passenger lists 1803–1806, on 399 pages, microfilms of which will be placed in our National Archives, Washington, D. C. These lists give name, age, town or parish of origin, and sometimes occupation and intended place of settlement in the United States; they concern Irish emigrants, mostly from the counties of Northern Ireland, about half of whom entered by the port of New York.[28]

The U. S. act of 1819 required shipmasters to submit to customs authorities lists of passengers, with the occupation, sex, and age of each. Country of allegiance and country (or town) of intended residence are also found on these lists. Such lists for the port of New York 1820–1919 are in the National Archives at Washington, D. C. Few are printed, but see:

U. S. Dep't of State: Letter from the secretary of state, with a transcript of the list of passengers who arrived in the United States from the 1st October 1819 to the 30th September 1820, printed 1821, 288 pp. (16th Congr., 2d Sess., Senate Doc. 118; serial 45), available at NYPL, Room 228, call No. *SBE/45.

NATURALIZATION

Naturalization by legislative act, one of the procedures in colonial times, was continued for a while. The 1777 constitution of New York State (Article XLII) said it shall be in the discretion of the legislature to naturalize all such persons and in such manner as they think proper, *if* they are born in parts beyond the sea and out of the United States, shall come to settle in and become subjects of this state and take oath of allegiance to this state and renounce all allegiance and subjection to every foreign potentate in all matters ecclesiastical and civil. A list of persons naturalized by acts of the State of New York, 1782–1789, is to be found in the O'Callaghan Papers, Box III, at NYHS. Or, consult the complete edition of *Laws of New York, 1777–1801*, republished 1886–87 by Weed, Parsons & Co. These naturalization acts are not in the early editions of the laws printed by Greenleaf and others, nor in the various General Indexes printed in the nineteenth century.

The U. S. act of 1790 passed by Congress was its first response to the Federal Constitution's granting it the power to establish a uniform rule of naturalization. It provided for the naturalization of free white aliens after two years' residence in the United States, upon application to any common law court of record in the state where they had resided for one year; minor children resident in the U. S. at the time became citizens also; any citizen already proscribed by a state was not to be readmitted to citizenship except by legislative act of the proscribing state. The stricter U. S. act of 1795, while reenacting these provisions concerning children and proscribed persons, required that (1) declaration of intention be sworn to in a state or federal court three years before naturalization, (2) when applying for citizenship, the alien swear he has resided five

---

[28]Mrs. Margaret Falley, in *The American Genealogist*, 28:243–44.

years in the U. S. and one year in the state or territory, and he renounces all foreign allegiance and will support the U. S. Constitution, (3) the court be satisfied of the applicant's residence, good moral character and attachment to the principles of the Constitution during said five years, and (4) any title or order of nobility be renounced. Except for the interval 1798–1802, the provisions of this 1795 act have, with slight changes, controlled the admission of foreign-born persons to citizenship in the United States.[29]

Naturalization records of the state courts of record for New York County (Supreme Court, Superior Court, Court of Common Pleas, and — before 1821 — Mayor's Court) start in 1792. They are under the New York County Clerk's jurisdiction and are now centralized with card index in Room 315, Supreme Court Building, 60 Centre St., New York, N. Y. Naturalization records of the Marine Court (organized 1806, name changed 1883 to the present name, City Court of New York) for the period 1806–1849 are under the City Court's jurisdiction, in Room 401, Old County Courthouse, Chambers St., New York, N. Y.

The U. S. District Court (organized 1789) did not exercise naturalization jurisdiction until 1824; its naturalization records for the period 1824–1906 are now located, together with card index, at the Immigration and Naturalization Service, U. S. Dep't of Justice, 70 Columbus Ave., New York, N. Y. This Service wrote me it has a consolidated index of all naturalizations in Greater New York prior to 1906.

Those declarations of intention required for naturalization that are under the jurisdiction of the New York County Clerk occupy many file cabinets in his office in the Hall of Records, Chambers St. They start in 1802 and consist of handwritten papers or filled-in forms, depending on the period; some are bound in libers by country of origin.

The following records evidently concern or include the declarations of intention necessary for citizenship applications.

In the Emmet Collection, MS Room of NYPL, is a "List of Immigrants 1802–1814" in early handwriting covering 7 pages,[30] from which I cull the column heads and the first entry:

Name	Birth place	Age	Nation	Allegiance	Country whence Emigrated	Place of intended Settlement	Date of Filing
George Cummings	Newry	34 yrs	Ireland	King of Gt. Br. & Irel'd	Hamburgh	State of New York	Oct. 29 1802

In NYSL are two series formerly in the Secretary of State's Office: Depositions of Resident Aliens 1825–1913 in 33 volumes with 3-volume index, and original signed documents bound as Alien Depositions 1825–1913 in 93 volumes. The amount of early

---

[29] "Legislative History of Naturalization in the U. S., 1776–1795", F. G. Franklin, in Amer. Hist'l Ass'n, *Annual Report for 1901*, 1:308–17.

[30] At the back of a thin 18th century folio listing New York Colony naturalizations by Oaths under Act of Parliament of 13th Year of King George II, reported annually to the Board of Trade; no indication of the court or official concerned in either list.

material is considerable, since the period into the year 1855 fills 12 volumes of the first series and 25 volumes of the second series. To cite an example of contents, the first item in both series may be summarized as: John Wright of New York City, starch manufacturer, depose that I am a native of Ireland and now live in New York City and intend to be a citizen as soon as I can be naturalized.

The preceding series of depositions were presumably started under the New York State law of 1825 (Chap. 307). This was an enabling act for any alien who has become an inhabitant of this state to take and hold real estate, providing he shall have made a written deposition before specified officials that he is a resident in and intends always to reside in the United States and to become a citizen thereof as soon as he can be naturalized and that he has taken such incipient measures as the United States laws require to obtain naturalization (under two provisos), such deposition to be filed in the Secretary of State's Office.

Most of the early New York laws on this subject granted certain aliens designated *by name* the right to buy and hold real estate "as any natural born citizen may or can do"; a few of these laws gave the aliens' residence or origin and family relationship, and a few (e.g. the 1823 law) limited such ownership to several years at which time the land was to revert to the state if such person were not by then a naturalized resident of the United States. A master list of the aliens named in these laws is printed in H. H. Havens' *General Index of the Laws of the State of New York 1777–1857*, pp. 31–73; the names cover the period 1789–1855 but occur mostly in 1789–1828. This printed list of aliens seems complete except for those in the 1811 law (Chap. 124) and an occasionally omitted individual, judging by my check of the laws 1777–1801 and spotcheck to 1813, after which date the list was compiled directly from the Statutes and so should be correct.

STATE AND FEDERAL CENSUS RECORDS

Numerous little-known statistical censuses were taken by the city and state in the period 1786–1821. Their statistics are to be found in *Minutes of the Common Council of the City of New York*, in *Census of the Electors and Total Population of the City and County of New York 1807*, printed by the City Inspector's Office (pamphlet at NYPL), and in the introduction to *Census of the State of New York for 1855*, Franklin B. Hough, 1857 (a large volume devoted entirely to statistics).

The state census of 1855 is far more important than the Federal censuses of the period. While the state took a regular census almost every ten years, unfortunately the only one still extant for New York County prior to that of 1905 is that of 1855. It is readily accessible in the New York County Clerk's Office, Room 703, Hall of Records, Chambers St., New York, N. Y.

The state census, taken June and July 1855, gives for each household: value of the dwelling, material of which it is built and number

34

of families occupying it; all members of a household by name, age, sex, and relation to the head of the family (wife, son, daughter, son-in-law, domestic, boarder, inmate, etc.); in what county of this state or in what other state or foreign country born; marital status; profession, trade or occupation; number of years resident in the city; whether native voter, naturalized voter, or alien; and whether an adult who cannot read or write.

The 1855 census takers used as census divisions the local election districts of each of the city's wards. This enables the present-day searcher to obtain a desired household faster than in a corresponding Federal census, since at the most only two or three election districts need be searched rather than an entire ward. While the bounds of the election districts were not set forth, the polling place of each of the 128 election districts in the 22 wards was published for the previous election (see N. Y. Times, issue of Nov. 7, 1854). The best procedure is to plot on a contemporary map (such as the 1854 fire insurance companies' map by Wm. Perris) both the desired household's home address taken from the city directory of 1855/6 and the various polling places of the ward within which the family address was situated, thereby ascertaining its probable election district from a pattern of the districting (if one shows up) or merely from proximity. Use of a contemporary map is important to ensure accuracy because of frequent changes in house-numbering as well as in street names. To cite an example, the address 197 W. 31 in 1855/6 was not in the 100 block as it would be today but in today's 300 block and the intervening two-block distance was enough to mean a different election district in 1855. One must beware against assuming that a modern-sounding address is the location it sounds like today.

The Federal censuses, taken every ten years, are at the National Archives, Washington, D. C., with respect to those of 1790 through 1870. They are complete for New York County. See "Transcript of Heads of Families listed in the Federal Census of New York County, 1800, with Indexes", Louis D. Scisco, 1924, MS at NYGB. With care this index may be used for the extra set of this county's 1800 Federal census (subscribed 1801), which is at NYHS and varies slightly in paging. See the forthcoming Supplement to this Guide for a listing of the items to be found in various Federal censuses for New York County.

The NYGB has just acquired a microfilm of the 1850 Federal census for New York County.

The census as of June 1, 1850 is the first Federal census *naming* all members of a household; it does *not* give their relationship or county of birth or some of the other data in the state census that can be so useful. The 1850 Federal census takers divided the city's wards into arbitrary divisions which did not correspond to local districting and the bounds of which are not now known. Hence search of an entire ward may be necessary. Sometimes it is possible to restrict the search and still be certain that a name was skipped by the census taker. Such instance occurs when the census-searcher spots the locality (by occasional comparison of names on the census with the same names and their addresses in the city's directory of 1850/1) and can follow the census-taker along the same side of the street past the desired address. The "hitch" is that he might only spot the other side of the street which might be in a different census division.

An aid to such procedure is Doggett's *New York City Street Directory for 1851*, which names householders along each street and can easily be translated into an 1850 list for at least some of the neighbours merely by comparison with one of the regular city directories of 1850/1 (by Rode or by Doggett). With care, it can be similarly used for the 1855 state census.

This 1851 street directory is especially useful as a double check both on one's interpretation of the sometimes incomplete address in the regular city directory and on one's calculations of the approximate location of the particular house number. The latter is so, because the street directory periodically breaks into its householders' lists with entries such as "here Amos St. intersects". An example of the former is the address "105 Fourth" in the 1850/1 city directory: I assumed it was not the present Fourth St. since no East or West was listed; a check in Stokes showed me that the old north-south Fourth St. had become Allen St. before that date; I did not like the idea of its being Fourth Avenue (on the city's east side) because the man's previous addresses had been on the city's west side; so I looked in the 1851 street directory, did not find my man in its Fourth Ave. listings but did find him in listings for a Fourth St.; whereupon I consulted the 1854 fire insurance maps and found 105 Fourth St. on the city's west side, part of the present Fourth St. not yet given its modern east and west numbering. If I had had the census searched for 105 Fourth Ave., results would have been negative since that location was in a different ward.

Another aid to census searching is the Runner's Vade Mecum, later called Street and Avenue Directory, which appears annually in the regular city directories starting 1827. It gives the house numbering at the street intersections: the 1827 to 1842 issues list the corner house numbers on either side of the intersecting street, while the issues from 1843 to after 1880 list the corner house numbers on either side of the designated street. This data was periodically revised to conform to new street names and new house numbering, and hence it is very helpful in dealing with the frequent changing in house numbering along various streets at unknown dates. It is our only aid (unless a contemporary map with house numbering is available) to pin-pointing a house for census searching, as is necessary when the particular street is the boundary between two or three wards.

The state electoral censuses form another group and are really lists of eligible voters, with some added statistics — mostly on kinds of wealth and property or on population totals, but *not* the size of individual households or the genealogical data usually brought to mind by the word census. I am inclined to feel that use of these censuses will be largely in connection with studying the relative wealth of individual families or of the higher economic classes. In this connection, see the tax lists and credit guides already mentioned under Wealth in the section Other Name Lists.

Six electoral censuses were taken between 1790 and 1821 under the first state constitution, as a basis for reapportioning senatorial and assembly districts. The qualifications of electors for representatives in the assembly were set by article VII of the State Constitution of 1777: "every male inhabitant of full age" (presumably white, colored, and Indian over 21 years old) who personally resided in one of the state's counties for the six months prior to election day *if* during that time he (1) possesses a freehold of £20 value or (2) has rented a tenement of 40 sh annual value and actually paid taxes to this state, and also the few freemen of Albany and New York City (as of 1775) actually resident in these cities.

The major statistics of the electoral censuses were printed by Hough, cited above. The manuscript libers giving names were imperfect before the 1911 Fire; salvaged portions are still at NYSL for the electoral censuses of 1801, 1814, and 1821 (but how much pertains to New York County has to be ascertained). The destroyed electoral census of 1807 is virtually replaced for the 3rd Ward of New York County by the 1808 list of its voters (electors) for the Assembly of 1809 (at NYHS), already mentioned in the Other Name Lists section of this Guide. Another set for the 1821 census is available in New York City: for the 1st, 2nd, 5th, 6th, 7th, and 9th Wards only of New York County, in MS booklets, now among the records of the Comptroller's Office.[31]

The 1821 census lists three groups of electors, as all male inhabitants who are citizens aged 21 or up *and* who (1) possess freeholds in the state valued at $250 and up, or (2) possess freeholds in the state valued at $50 to $250, or (3) rent tenements of $5 annual value. It also lists another large category (see Hough for details) who became voters the next year under the new constitution. The totals for New York County are 16,659 male electors and 3,266 specified other males aged at least 21 years for a grand total of 19,925. To provide a very rough idea of the proportion of the populace who were then electors (voters), the closest comparable statistics of general population in the 1820 Federal census of the county are 21,331 free white males aged 26 and over or 32,348 free white males aged 16 and over.[32] With respect to the 1821 electoral census set in the Comptroller's Office, names are confined to the column "head of each family and of jurors", the remainder being the number in each family qualifying in the above four categories and as jurors, number of improved acres, cattle, mills, etc.

---

[31] For access to Comptroller's records, see comment in note 25.

[32] For published tables of Federal census statistics, see *Checklist of U. S. Public Documents, 1789–1909,* 3rd ed., Government Printing Office, 1911, pp. 445–6.

MAPS, STREET, AND LAND RECORDS

Maps are so very important for this period that I doubt if a thorough search can be made without recourse to them. Early nineteenth century maps of the city show names and locations of many of the big landowners, churches, cemeteries, and other institutions — an example is the 1836 map reproduced in Stokes' *Iconography of Manhattan Island*, III:plate 99. Such maps can be put to good use in orienting the searcher to the streets of the period and in helping him determine, for instance, what church records to search, since the poor transportation facilities of the period usually resulted in a person's attending a church near his home. The property survey map and the re-indexed block maps may provide a clue, if only by naming adjoining landowners. Small city maps, useful especially in showing ward boundaries for census work, are in *Valentine's Manuals*. One should never fail to consult Stokes' *Iconography*.

The best usable collections of maps, ranging from atlases to private surveys of individual properties, are at NYHS, NYPL, and the Register's Office. *Manhattan Maps, a Co-operative List*, Daniel C. Haskell (reprint from NYPL *Bulletin* for 1930) lists maps in four libraries and some city departments, by years 1600–1930. Of the following maps, all available at NYHS, the first three are especially good for identifying country houses of individuals and institutions:

1811 *Map of the City of New York by the Commissioners* under the 1807 act, John Randel, Jr., surveyor (his original notebooks and surveys are at NYHS).

1851 *Plan of N.Y.C.*, based on surveys, pub. Mathew Dripps, 1851.

1867 *Plan of N.Y.C.*, based on surveys, pub. Mathew Dripps, 1867.
(Both series show lots and buildings, house numbers at block corners, old farm lines, and names of many uptown owners.)

Maps of various sections of Manhattan, J. B. Holmes, city surveyor, pub. 1865–1887 (the basis of titles of that period: include old farm and boundary lines, subdivisions, and notes on land transfers of the previous 100 years).

Atlases of various wards of Manhattan surveyed for fire insurance companies, Wm. Perris, surveyor, later Perris & Browne, pub. 1852–1889 (do not give ownership but at periodic printing dates show each building, its nature and house numbering).

The map room of the Register's Office of New York County is Room 104 in the Hall of Records, Chambers St. Here are some 5,200 filed maps, about 5,000 maps copied from conveyance libers, thousands of maps copied from various public offices of the city, a large number of maps copied from Valentine, Tuttle, Hoffman, Innes and printed atlases, many maps reconstructed from descriptions in old conveyances or old maps platted on present street lines, and maps of parcels of land laid out in building lots.[33] Also here is a card index of maps by street location. Much of this work was done by the department in the period 1911–1917. See also *Descriptive Index of the Maps on record in the Office of the Register of the City and County of New York*, Adolf Dengler, 1875. For further discussion, see other paragraphs of this section.

The constant change in street names, especially in lower Manhattan, is a problem in census and land work — and also in biographical research, for which a good knowledge of local addresses is a great help in eliminating other people of the same name from continuing consideration. In 1811 Manhattan Island was laid out by the Commissioners in the present rectangular gridiron system, but there were many local changes in direction and location of streets before and after that date. Stokes' *Iconography* is the most reliable, useful, and convenient source if it has the desired

---

[33] Stokes, VI:216–18, which gives further details.

data; he includes the date of change but only a partial list of streets. Post is the overall handy compendium listing streets by old and new names, but the many streets bearing the same name for some unstated short period during two centuries are often confusing since he does not give the date of name change. Many of the early directories and guides of the city include a list of streets, giving their names, extent, and direction at that time. Dunshee's book has many charts of blocks in lower Manhattan, showing: physical changes in the direction, extent and width of streets, sometimes as many as three systems of house numbering prevailing at different specified dates, and the houseowners in a specified year. The master index of the *Minutes of the Common Council* makes this the most convenient of the city's records to consult; it includes a list of names of the streets, alleys and lanes of the city. See also the last paragraph of this section.

1794   Account of the Alterations of the Names of Several of the Streets in the City of New York, in Duncan's 1794 directory.
1799   *New-York Register and City Directory*, Longworth, 1799.
1805   *New-York Mercantile and General Directory for . . . 1805–6*, Jones.
1807   *Alphabetical Table of Streets . . . Public Buildings . . . of New York*, John Low, 1807.
1811   *New-York Directory for the Year 1811*, Elliot & Crissy.
1827   *Description of the City of New-York*, James Hardie.
1836   *Guide to the City of New York; containing an alphabetical list of streets, etc., accompanied by a correct map*, pr. J. Disturnell, 1836.
Old Streets . . . of New York, Showing the Former and Present Names, John J. Post, 1882.
As You Pass By, Kenneth Holcomb Dunshee, 1952 (appx: Directory of Forgotten Streets).
Card index of streets by old name and by modern name, with date of name change and occasional data on the street (complete for Manhattan and partial for other boroughs): at Municipal Reference Library, Room 2230, Municipal Building, Chambers St., N.Y.C.
Card index of streets by locations and giving dates of origin, etc.: at Division of Design, Office of President of the Borough of Manhattan, Room 2136, Municipal Building, Chambers St., N.Y.C. (permission required).

The unheralded change in house numbering is a difficult problem to overcome; it occurs at unknown and varying dates on different streets to the present day. If an exactly contemporary survey map is unavailable, refer to the city directories after 1827; the other sources listed below give householders at numbers along designated streets. See discussion in the Census section of this Guide.

1827 — after 1880   Runner's Vade Mecum later called Street and Avenue Directory, annual and periodically revised section of the regular N.Y.C. directories (e.g. Rode's newly compiled June 1, 1850 and Trow's corrected to May 1, 1880): gives under each street name the intersecting streets and house numbering at the corners.
1812   *Improved New-York Double Directory for 1812*, Elliot.
1851   *New York City Street Directory for 1851*, Doggett.
1874, 1877   *Directory of the Registered Voters of the City of New York arranged by streets and house numbers*, Davenport, at NYPL (1874 ed.: streets grouped by wards, assembly and election districts).
1874–1902   *Élite Private Address and Carriage Directory*, Phillips.

A full set of land conveyance libers for Manhattan since 1683, of mortgage libers since 1754, and of power of attorney libers since 1825 are in the Office of the Register of New York County. This office was created in 1812, previous to which these records were under the County Clerk. Although the sets of libers are complete, many deeds were recorded with the Secretary of State until the act of 1811, requiring that deeds affecting New York County property be filed in the County Clerk's office. Hence for the early period one should also consult records of the Land Office at Albany (under the Secretary of State).[34] This can often be done through: *An Essay towards an Improved Register of Deeds, City and County of New-York to Dec. 31, 1799 inclusive*, Charles F. Grim, N. Y. 1832, which includes an "Index of Deeds in the Office of the Secretary of State that relate to lands in the City and County of New York, as so lettered".

The chronological deed libers and mortgage libers (old series in Room 101 and mezzanine respectively, with a printed index of grantees and grantors in Room 104) are the type familiar to searchers in the eastern states. While the practice of giving genealogical data in such records gradually fell into disuse, I have found as late as a deed of 1811 relationships, residences, and occupations, those living and deceased, of two generations of a family in which one of the sisters married a man of the same surname, being sale of a moiety of lands in the Western District of the state promised her deceased brother for his services as a private in the New York Line of the Revolutionary army.[35]

The uniqueness and remarkable usability of the Register's Office records is highlighted in those instances in which the searcher knows the approximate modern location of the property and wishes to follow the history of that property (either for itself or as a means of learning more about the owning family). Under acts of 1889, 1910, and 1912, the deeds, open mortgages, and various encumbrances have been abstracted and indexed by locality. This additional system of recording, often referred to as the block and section system (sections abolished in 1917), is in Rooms 203 and 204, which also have for ready reference key a street index of lower Manhattan and a large scale modern map of Manhattan on racks, giving the official number of each block. Every block on Manhattan Island has been given an official number, corresponding to numbers on the tax maps; each block has also been subdivided into numbered lots for easier identification on the records, but it must be cautioned that these lot numbers are unofficial and, although the same as the tax lots, are *not* the same as the house numbers appearing along the streets and in directories. Under this system, all records for a particular block can be readily found in a binder

---

[34] Good card indexes are in the Land Office, Albany. Card indexes of deeds (about 1,400) and of patents relating to N. Y. C. at Albany were in the Register's Office, N. Y. C., in 1927 (Stokes, VI:219) but seem to be unknown there now; presumably they may now be in the locked storeroom in the mezzanine.
The Land Office is now at 164 State St., Albany.

[35] Recorded in 1815 in New York County Deeds 110:185.

for the period 1917–1937 or in the current binder, both entitled Block Index Conveyances, while all identified open records for that block prior to 1917 can be readily found in a similar binder, an unofficial index entitled Re-Indexed Conveyances prior to 1917.

The last-named index is of most interest to genealogist and historian. Theoretically it goes back to 1654, date of the earliest deed book. Actually, despite much research and reconstruction (alluded to in the foregoing map paragraph), about one-fifth of deeds prior to 1891 were not identified sufficiently to place them surely within a modern block, and about four-fifths of the mortgages had been closed and so were not entered on this Re-Index. Hence one must not accept at face value entries such as "no instruments of record 1654–1805" or "1798–1803 and 1807–1820". But for the period covered by this Guide, this Re-Index usually has sufficient or most of the information. The binder contains a map of the block with its lotting, followed by chronological entries of the records under the headings: grantor, grantee, date of record, liber and page, index lot no. where known (otherwise entered as unlotted), and remarks.

Many of the blocks in the Re-Indexed Conveyances start with summary of early ownership as a farm or with reference to an early division in family ownership. In such event the searcher, who wishes to trace back in time, goes to the Map Room and consults the Tract Reports Block Index, which gives the blocks for which tract (farm) reports have been compiled; generally speaking, these are the blocks north of 23rd Street. These histories of the older farms are not confined to Register's Office records but include wills, judgments in partition suits, etc., showing development of a farm from the earliest patent or deed to the time when the farm was conveyed in small parcels under the present street system. They include diagrams locating the farm and its sub-divisions and charts summarizing the development of the title to the late owners when the farm was divided by streets.[36]

The searcher can obtain some land data and desired official block numbers by studying Stokes' *Iconography*, especially Vol. VI, which has: a map, in many sections, of original grants and farms, drawn superimposed on a modern map of Manhattan Island showing both present-day streets and the Register's Office number of each block; also on pp. 65–177 a study by Jennie F. Macarthy of Original Grants and Farms, which in some instances is carried down into the period of this Guide. Other especially important printed studies (including maps) are the following first two items:

Abstracts of Farm Titles in the City of New York, between 39th and 120th Streets, East Side, and between 39th and 73rd Streets West of the Common Lands, H. Croswell Tuttle, 1877–81 in 3 vols.

Abstract of Title of Kip's Bay Farm in the City of New York, John J. Post, 1894, 2056 pp. (covers the region 26th to 42nd Sts. and 1st Ave. to Lexington Ave.).

Abstract of all Conveyances, Leases, Releases, etc. . . . made by the Mayor, Aldermen and Commonalty of . . . (N.Y.C., 1682 to) *1872; Supplement . . . 1872–1882*, John S. Ames, late Searcher, 1872 and 1882 at NYPL (has index by streets).

[36]Stokes. VI:218

Special land records resulting from the wars of the period are listed in the Military Records section of this Guide.

A specialist may need to consult maps, street, and land records in other departments of the city. I shall only summarize here what seems most likely to be useful, all but the last item taken from Paltsits' 1927 bibliography.[37] In many instances, the location and the department in charge may be different now or soon, and records may be difficult of access, so written inquiries should be made before the material is needed.

Index of Maps filed in the office of the Street Commissioner, 1763–1838 (alphabetical): No. 203, Dep't of Finance.

Names of streets and avenues opened, 1824–1844: No. 913, Dep't of Finance.

City Grants 1686–1907 in 10 libers: Division of Real Estate, Dep't of Finance (mainly lots along the water front, partly or wholly under water at time of grant).

Common lands — adjustment of boundary lines, and lots sold by the city 1795–1825: at *ibid*.

Accounts of Street openings in 4 libers; cessions to the city from private parties of land needed for opening streets 1759–1858 in 1 liber: Division of Design (formerly the Engineer of Street Openings) under President of Borough of Manhattan.

Important collection of maps especially relating to streets: at *ibid*.

Original record of assessments prepared by the Tax Department 1808–1930, in maps and libers, showing the individual owner's name, valuation, unimproved and improved lots: now in the Municipal Archives and Records Center, 238 William St.

BURIAL RECORDS AND CEMETERIES

The frequent question, Where are the burial remains of such a person? can seldom be answered with certainty for a New York City death before 1850. Almost no cemeteries remain in the old New York City other than Trinity Churchyard, Trinity Cemetery uptown, St. Paul's Churchyard, the Marble Cemeteries, and parts of two Jewish cemeteries. Records of removal of remains from the many former cemeteries are usually poor; the city did not keep reburial records although permits occasionally appear on the city council minutes, and while records of the individual church or cemetery may include note of removals, in many instances the specific remains were unidentifiable at the time of removal.

In the early nineteenth century, the rapid increase in population soon filled the old churchyards and led to the opening of new cemeteries in the then outskirts, usually in the region between Houston, North (now East Houston), and 12th Streets. Expansion of the populated area also led to the building of uptown churches, sometimes with vaults and burial yards. The city's concern for health resulted in progressive restriction of burials in the populous area. An 1823 ordinance (repassed 1827 and 1839) forbade all burials in grave or vault south of Canal, Sullivan, and Grand Sts. On Feb. 3, 1851 the city amended this ordinance,

---

[37] See Stokes, VI:201, 202, 207, and other pages for other records of possible interest. See also my notes 20 & 25, and description of the Municipal Archives and Records Center project in the Special Records and Archives section of this Guide.

forbidding interments south of 86th Street except in private vaults and cemeteries, and prohibiting establishment of any new cemetery in New York County.[38] This ordinance and the high real estate value of Manhattan property resulted in sale of most cemeteries and removal of the bodies to new religious and, especially, to new non-sectarian cemeteries, established in adjoining counties but now within greater New York City limits. The earliest of these is Green-Wood Cemetery in Kings County,[39] where burials started in 1842.

Although the present location of remains is often undeterminable, many of the churches and modern cemeteries[40] have excellent old burial records, sexton's records, or interment records, some chronological and some alphabetical, giving a varying amount of information on the deceased. One point to remember in using the excellent Trinity Parish burial records is that part of the old Wall St. churchyard was the accepted burial place for strangers in the city.

The following incomplete list of Manhattan's cemeteries *other than* churchyards is an attempt to fill the need for such a list. St. John's Cemetery given below was a cemetery for the churches of Trinity Parish and is not to be confused with one of them — St. John's Chapel at Varick and Laight Sts. (records do not indicate burial in its church grounds). The asterisk against a date denotes mass removal of bodies but does not preclude earlier individual removals.

Denomination	Cemetery[40]	Cemetery Use or Ownership[41]	Location of Cemetery
Baptist	First Church	1815–1861*	E. Houston bet: 1st and 2nd Aves.
Catholic[42]		1801–1833	Mott and Prince Sts.
		1828–1848	Middle Rd., now 5th Ave. and 50th St.
	St. Patrick's	1832–1913	11th St. bet: 1st Ave. and Ave. A.
Episcopal	St. John's	1801–1896*	Hudson and Clarkson Sts., Greenwich Village; now Jas. J. Walker Park
	Trinity, uptown	1842–now	153rd St. and Amsterdam Ave.
	St. Mark's	1806–	12th St. bet: 1st and 2nd Aves.
	St. Stephen's	c1810–	1st St. bet: 1st and 2nd Aves.
Jewish	Shearith Israel	1655–1855*	New Bowery near Oliver St.
		1805–1833	Milligan, now 72 W. 11th St.
		1829–1851	21st St. bet: 6th and 7th Aves.
	Bnai Jeshurun	c1827–1857*	32nd St. bet: 6th and 7th Aves.
Lutheran		c1800–1869*	Carmine St., Greenwich Village
Methodist Epis.		1805–1855	1st St., NW corner of 2nd Ave.
Moravian		1754–1816*	Mott and Pell Sts.
		c1816–1871*	Orchard St.
Presbyterian	First Church	1807–1865	E. Houston and Forsyth Sts.
	Brick Church	1807/9–1865*	E. Houston and Chrystie Sts.
	Rutgers Church	1807/9–1866	E. Houston and Forsyth Sts.
	Scotch Church 2nd Associate Ref. }	–1832	at NE end of present Washington Square; Wooster St.
	Scotch Church	1827–	28th St.
	2nd Associate	1842–1852	E. Houston and Forsyth Sts.
	2nd Reformed	c1843–1858c	41st St. west of 9th Ave.
	Irish Church	–1853*	25th St. east of 9th Ave.

---

[38] *Minutes of the Common Council,* III:462, XII:811, XVI:136; *By-Laws and Ordinances,* revised 1839. *By-Laws and Ordinances,* revised 1845; *Revised Ordinances,* 1856.

[39] *Green-Wood Cemetery, Catalogue of Proprietors, to Aug. 1, 1884* (1884) at NYHS (alphabetical list of owners of 24,758 lots). More useful than MS of Greenwood Cemetery inscriptions which covers only a small portion.

[40] For burial records and gravestone inscriptions, see Church Records section. At NYHS are *inter alia* the records of both the Marble Cemeteries, interments of Market St. Dutch Church 1835 on, and MS of gravestone inscriptions of Trinity Cemetery, uptown. At NYGB are MS copies of Trinity Parish burial records 1777 on and gravestone inscriptions.

[41] Information largely from New York County deeds located through study of the 1836 map of the city in Stokes and of the 1851 Dripps map.

[42] All started as separate cemeteries, but the old St. Patrick's Church soon built on the Mott St. ground; ending dates confused: U. S. Cath. Hist. Soc. *Historical Records & Studies,* 1:369.

44

Denomination	Cemetery	Cemetery Use or Ownership	Location of Cemetery
Quaker		1796–1874*	E. Houston and Chrystie Sts
Reformed	Dutch	1796–1874*	E. Houston and Forsyth Sts.
	German	–1846*	12th St.
Non-sectarian	African (negro)	1795–1853	Chrystie St. near Stanton St.
Episcopal	St. Philips: 1827		
Non-sectarian	Marble Cemetery	1832–	2nd Ave. bet: 2nd and 3rd Sts.
Non-sectarian	N. Y. C. Marble Cemetery	1832–	2nd St. bet: 1st and 2nd Aves.
Non-sectarian?[43]		1845–1852	45th St. bet: 10th and 11th Aves.
City cemeteries	Potter's Field Bellevue Hospital		Many of them; see Stokes

A useful mid-century list of churches with their address, sexton and burial grounds is to be found in Doggett's *New York City and Co-Partnership Directory for 1843 & 1844*, pp. 413–17. The burial places listed under the surname letters B and C in Death Register No. 1 have been classified in the tables on religious affiliation given below. While of interest, they must be interpreted with care, not only because certain groups had a much higher death rate than others (for example, the Irish immigrant on a low economic level was more liable to consumption, then the highest cause of adult deaths) but also because with registration a new matter dependent on cooperation of sextons, many of the new and loosely-knit church groups probably overlooked registration and it is evident (from the church table at the end of this Guide) that few of the churches in the rural sections reported.

Denomination of the Cemetery (including Churchyards)	1801–1814 Burials filed with the City	Evident* Number of Cemeteries reporting	Birth place	Religious Breakdown of the Large Foreign-Born Groups				
				Cath-olic	Epis-copal	Presby-terian	Other **	Potters Field
Baptist	27	3						
Catholic	159	1						
Congregational	—	—	England		27		7	11
Disciples Christ	—	—	France					
Episcopal	389	8	and West				5	6
Jewish	1	1	Indies					
Lutheran	39	2	Ireland	58	18	10		40
Methodist	93	3	Scotland			10	4	7
Moravian	3	1						
Presbyterian	172	10						
Quaker	40	1						
Reformed	140	9						
Universalists	7	1	*highly tentative.					
African (negro)	159	4						
Public	392	2	**not classified by me when groups small.					

MILITARY RECORDS

Military records for this 1783–1855 period are few and scattered. Family data, birthplace, age, and residence may be found sometimes in the pension papers and bounty land papers of patriot American soldiers for the Revolutionary War and for the War of 1812, in the National Archives at Washington, D. C. In the manuscript room of the NYPL are the claims of losses by the loyalists in the Revolution; family data to be occasionally found in these papers may also be useful since many loyalist families returned to the New York area. Military records of the War of 1812 at Washington are in the custody of the Old Records Section, Office of the Adjutant General, Dep't of the Army, National Archives

---

[43] See New York County Deeds 500:95, etc.

Building. They include historical summaries of 303 New York military units, describing muster, pay and other rolls in the collection, card indexed. New York State's War of 1812 military records were sent to Washington before 1900;[44] evidently they have been amalgamated with the foregoing, though seemingly no evidence to this effect. In the Adjutant General's office at Albany for this period are merely military indices or registers of officers 1803–1813, 1831–1846 and from 1847 on, also some copies of payrolls of New York troops in the War of 1812. Special land records resulting from the wars are included with military records, military units and pension lists given below.

Historical Register of the U. S. Army . . . 1789 to 1889, F. B. Heitman, 1890.

List of Officers of the Army of the U. S. from 1779 to 1900, Col. Wm. H. Powell, U. S. A., 1900.

General Register of the U. S. Navy and Marine Corps . . . 1782 to 1882, Thos. H. S. Hamersley, 1882.

List of Officers of the Navy of the U. S. and of the Marine Corps from 1775 to 1900, Edward W. Callahan, 1901.
> (Above four titles on this list concern officers and often give deathdates, the army ones giving birthplaces.)

Military Minutes of the Council of Appointment of the State of New York, 1783–1821, 4 vols., 1901 (original minutes still exist from 1786 and are now at NYSL).

Officers of New York State Militia; New York City and Vicinity 1786–1822, Norman F. Cushman, 1946, MS in 2 vols. at NYHS.

1786–1836 Rosters of Officers from the records at Albany, 1 vol., at NYHS.

"Partial Bibliography of Printed Works which contain records of Service in the War of 1812 . . .", Hy. H. Noble, pp. 48–54 of *General Society of the War of 1812: Proceedings . . . at Phila., 1912.*

Index to American Prisoners of the War of 1812, in *News-Letter*, National Society, U. S. Daughters of 1812, v. 13, #4 (1938), etc., at NYHS (name, number and birthplace of prisoners received at Quebec as recorded in General Entry Book, Public Archives of Canada at Ottowa) (original records cover prisoners of land and naval forces, privateers and merchant ships, with age, capture, discharge, death, etc.; certified copy at Library of Congress).

The Prisoners' Memoirs, or Dartmoor Prison [Charles Andrews], N. Y. 1852, at NHYS (pp. 138–51: lists of American prisoners 1813–15 who were imprisoned at Dartmoor, at Stapleton and on prisonships at Chatham, deathdates of those who died there, those who escaped, and those impressed from there into His Majesty's service, with their birthplace or former residence and the ships from which they were captured or impressed) (many from New York).

Public Papers of Daniel D. Tompkins, Governor of New York, ed. Hugh Hastings, 3 vols. 1898–1904.

New York and Vicinity during the War of 1812–15, R. S. Guernsey, 2 vols., 1889.

War of 1812 Index of service records at Albany by F. G. Mather, 3 boxes at NYHS.

War of 1812 Military roll of officers, payrolls, muster rolls in 1 package, 2 vols., and 4 boxes at NYHS; also orderly books there.

War of 1812 Records in 25 vols., formerly at State Comptroller's Office, now at NYSL (largely historical, but include accounts of the paymasters and commissaries during the war and some enlistment papers in the Corps of Sea Fencibles, org. 1813).

1836–1846 Military fines: Adjutant General's records now at NYSL.

---

[44] See statement in *Military Minutes, op. cit* (1901), p. 61, and negative evidence in Osgood, *op. cit.* (1900), 2:126.

History of the Mexican War, General Cadmus M. Wilcox, 1892 (rosters of army officers, of volunteer officers, and of navy officers by ships).

A Complete Roster of the Regular and Volunteer Troops in the War between the United States and Mexico, from 1846 to 1848, Wm. Hugh Robarts, 1887 at NYHS (officers only, arranged by states).

Official List of Officers who marched with the Army under . . . Major General Winfield Scott, from Puebla upon the City of Mexico . . . and were engaged in the battles of Mexico, 1848 at NYHS (includes N. Y. volunteers and some deathdates).

Reports of the Special Committees . . . for bringing on from Mexico the bodies of the officers of the New York Regiment of Volunteers and to . . . present Medals to (this Regiment) *. . . on their return from Mexico* [N. Y. Common Council], 1850 at NYPL and NYHS (biographical sketches of 5 officers killed and rolls of the 11 companies, including those discharged and dead, of First Regiment of N. Y. Volunteers) (different unit from the following).

California Expedition: Stevenson's Regiment of First New York Volunteers, Guy J. Griffen, 1951 at NYPL (alphabetical list of regiment's members 1846–48 with brief biographical data including deaths).

Institution of the Society of the Cincinnati, formed by the officers of the American Army of the Revolution, 1783 . . . The New York State Society, John Schuyler, 1886 (gives membership rolls of 1784, 1788 and 1886, with biographies of original members and lines of descent to the 1886 members).

Roster of Veteran Corps of Artillery, New York, Constituting the Military Society War of 1812, Norman F. Cushman, MS in 2 vols. at NYGB (gives members 1790–1890 alphabetically by name, with address and military service) (This corps was organized 1790 in N. Y. C. by officers and soldiers of the Revolution as an active independent military corps to guard the city; it was the first to volunteer in 1812).

Veteran Corps of Artillery Military Society of the War of 1812: miscellaneous records, scrapbooks, etc., at NYHS (see description in NYHS *Annual Report* for 1950).

History of the Seventh Regiment of New York, 1806–1889, Emmons Clark, 1890 in 2 vols.

Washington Grays (cavalry unit org. 1833 N. Y. C.) enrollment book and material on, 1837–1879, collection of its colonel, together with data on New York military history: DeVoe papers in 5 vols. at NYHS.

New York, The World's Metropolis, 1623-4—1923-4, Wm. T. Bonner, 1924 (includes paragraphs on numerous military units and leaders).

List of military organizations, in Stokes' *Iconography*, VI:490–92.

Transcripts of the Manuscript Books and Papers of the Commission of Enquiry into losses and services of American Loyalists, 1783–1790, MS in 60 vols. at NYPL (This collection includes the sessions at both Nova Scotia and London; the New York City cases are primarily in vols. 17–24, 29–31 and 41–46).

Record of Sales by the Commissioners of Forfeiture, 1784–1787, liber now in Room 209, Register's Office, Hall of Records, Chambers St., New York. (It contains a descriptive list of estates of American Loyalists in the Southern District of New York which were confiscated and sold, together with the purchasers, the most complete known to exist for any section of the state according to Professor Flick. For a tabulation of this liber, see his *Loyalism in New York during the American Revolution*, 1901).

Abstracts of the foregoing liber and a box of papers concerning forfeited estates 1784–1790, at NYHS.

Disposition of Loyalist Estates in the Southern District of the State of New York, Harry B. Yoshpe, 1939 (includes bibliography of manuscript sources and appendices of sales and of claims, including those who suffered losses whose estates were not confiscated).

1764–1775, 1790–1797 Military patents at Land Office, Albany.

1817–1818 Land grants to soldiers: Adjutant General's records now at NYSL.

The Balloting Book, and Other Documents relating to Military Bounty Lands in the State of New-York, 1825 (the state's bounties for Revolutionary War services).

Invalids of the Revolution pensioned by New York State, and applicants: lists on pp. 551–53 of *New York in the Revolution*, Berthold Fernow, 1887, and on pp. 271–73 of *New York in the Revolution as Colony and State*, James A. Roberts, 1898; abstracts in O'Callaghan Papers, Box III, at NYHS of the Comptroller's Books A & D Invalid Pensions (certificates issued 1779–1786 giving service, wound, and very seldom a birth or death date and widow); 4 boxes of alphabetically arranged depositions and certificates now at NYSL.

Index of Awards on Claims of the Soldiers of the War of 1812, as audited and allowed by the Adjutant and Inspector Generals (of N. Y., under) . . . *Laws of 1859*, Albany, 1860 (gives residence by town, county and state).

Index to Revolutionary War Pension Applications: Supplement to National Genealogical Society Quarterly, starting March 1943 (alphabetical full name index of soldiers and sailors or their widows who applied for federal pensions or bounty lands, and the state from which each served, with disposition of claim, in the official files of the National Archives).

Letter from the Secretary of the Navy, accompanying a report of the Commissioners of the Fund for Navy pensioners, 1804 at NYPL (lists navy pensioners by state and rank).

Letter from the Secretary of War, communicating a transcript of the pension list of *the United States*, 1813 (reprinted in *Collections of the Minnesota Historical Society*, 6:503–39), reprint 1953 (master alphabetical list for each state of pensions for disability in service).

Letter from the Secretary of War, transmitting a Report of the Names, Rank and Line of every Person placed on the Pension List . . . (under) *Act of 1818* (1820) (Revolutionary War pensioners on rolls by state of residence; a few death dates).

Report from the Secretary of War . . . (on) *the Pension Establishment of the United States*, 3 vols., 1835 (gives in groups by county of residence: name, rank, service, age and many deathdates of pensioners qualifying as invalid or under the 1818 and 1832 acts basic for the Revolutionary War, also representatives of those benefitting under the 1828 act and heirs of those who obtained 5 years half-pay in lieu of bounty land under the 1816 act) (many New York County pensioners shown with services from other states).

Census of Pensioners for Revolutionary or Military Services, with their names, ages and places of residence . . ., 1841 (pensioner and head of family with whom he lived 1840, grouped by residence in N. Y. C. wards or other census districting; no service given but mostly the Revolution).

List of Pensioners on the Roll January 1, 1883, giving the name of each pensioner, the cause for which pensioned, the post-office address . . ., 5 vols., 1883 (seldom shows the war, but mostly War of 1812 soldiers and their widows under the basic acts of 1871 and 1878 for this war) (only Civil War and Mexican War pensions based on death or disability in service).

Veterans' Administration, Its History, Activities and Organization, Gustavus A. Weber and Laurence F. Schmeckebier, 1934 at NYPL (has good study of 19th century pension and bounty land laws) (the non-current pension and bounty land files have since been transferred from the V.A. to the National Archives).

For pension and other claims against the U. S. Government, see also Federal Records section of this Guide.

SPECIAL RECORDS AND ARCHIVES

The Iconography of Manhattan Island, 1498–1909, in 6 oversize volumes, by I. N. Phelps Stokes is a basic source even for the late period of this Guide. It is compiled entirely from original documents. It contains maps, views, land records, history, and a chronology of big and little events. Its Index, Vol. VI, pp. 287–677, is really a study of many subjects and is invaluable for many purposes, from picking up an item on or obtaining the exact name of a little-known institution to finding dates of changes in street names and in ward boundaries. The Bibliography of fundamental sources of New York City history by the eminent Victor H. Paltsits, 1928, occupies pp. 178–282 of Vol. VI; it consists primarily of detailed reports on the archives for Manhattan of many departments of the city and county, it includes unprinted documents in libraries throughout the nation, and it has an extensive list of secondary sources, frequently evaluated. For additional guides to archives, see Secondary and Other Sources section of this Guide.

The Municipal Archives and Records Center of the New York Public Library is downtown in the Rhinelander Building, 238 William Street, New York, N. Y., in charge of James Katasaros, Supervisor. This is a relatively new project, in the stage of educating city officials to the benefits of centralizing their records. It is open to the public, and the accessibility of the records under its control makes it a boon to researchers in municipal records. It has two divisions: the records center, for storing inactive records of

New York City agencies and departments, and the municipal archives, for maintaining New York City documents of historical value. The latter division contains as yet only (1) the voluminous papers of the Mayor's Office (both the old records described in Stokes, VI:189–191, and later records); (2) the original record of assessments prepared by the Tax Department 1808–1930, in maps and libers, showing the individual owner's name, valuation, unimproved and improved lots; and (3) New York City newspapers 1835 to date, formerly in the County Clerk's Office; and it is in process of receiving (4) many of the records of the City Clerk's Office (described in Stokes, VI:185–189), though which are to be transferred has not yet been decided.

THE COURTS

Records of most civil courts in the county are at the New York County Clerk's Office, Hall of Records, Chambers St., New York, N. Y. It is questionable how useful they are to the researcher without legal training and knowledge of old legal terms, especially as the minute books, etc., are poorly indexed, if at all (often only by chief plaintiff).[45] Readily useful though are this office's card indexes of the loose papers under its jurisdiction. Some of these card indexes are mentioned elsewhere in this Guide. Others are: Court of Common Pleas (called Mayor's Court before 1821) Judgments and Orders 1786 on, Superior Court Judgments 1828–1895, Supreme Court Special Proceedings 1847–1885, Pleadings (Supreme Court and Co. Clerk's misc. papers of 18th century and up to 1847; only pleadings after 1847), and Miscellaneous file 1812–1934. While the County Clerk has many records of both the old Supreme Court of Judicature and the Court of Chancery (resp. reorganized or abolished 1847), the better part of their records are now with the Clerk of the Court of Appeals, at Eagle St., Albany; alphabetical indexes are available for many of the papers and for some of the libers.[45]

Indices to Notices of Suits in Equity, filed in the Office of the Clerk of the City and County of New-York 1823–1855, 8 vols., 1857, at NYPL and NYHS (all defendants of the name in a suit listed together, with complainants' names opposite: alphabetical index of defendants).

Indices of Judgments; docketed in the City and County of New York . . . 1844–1855, 25 vols., 1857 at NYHS (in the various civil courts).

Index to Wills, Deeds, and Other Instruments, and to Litigations affecting the Title to Real Property which have been judicially considered by the Courts of the State of New York, Frederick H. Comstock, 1896, at NYPL (covers the reports of cases decided by the courts, giving the citations).

Treatise on the practice of the Supreme Court of the State of New York, Claudius L. Monell, 2d ed., 2 vols., 1853–54: at N. Y. C. Bar Assn. Library.

Jurisdiction and records of some of the above courts in relation to estates and heirs have been discussed in the Probate and Related Records section of this Guide. That section deals fully with the Court of Probates and the Surrogate's Court.

[45] See critical comment in Greene & Morris' Guide to Sources, p. 209.
For details on court records at both offices, see Stokes, VI:212–16, and Osgood, 1900, 2:129–31.

There are many other courts whose records, as a rule, will not concern the genealogist or biographer. Descriptions of the records of many such courts are given in Stokes, in Osgood, in Greene & Morris, and in Goebel & Naughton. I believe most of their records are now in the new Federal Courts building (U. S. Court House, Foley Square), the city's new Criminal Courts building (at 100 Centre St.) and Old County Court Building (in City Hall Park). The old Police Department records were thrown away, the oldest remaining dating from 1845.[46]

City Civil Appointments and Administration

The city's many appointed and elected officials and the city administration are sometimes hard to obtain desired records of without knowledge of the fact and approximate date, except in the period 1784–1831, for which there is a master index of the *Minutes*. Some officials of the city and county of New York appear in Werner's indexed civil list of the state. Biographical sketches of many city officeholders are to be found in Bonner's history and in Valentine's manuals.

Minutes of the Common Council of the City of New York, 1784–1831, pr. 1917–18 (has excellent detailed master index in 2 vols.).

Proceedings of the Board of Aldermen of the City of New York, 1831–1897 in 228 vols.

Proceedings of the Boards of Aldermen and Assistant Aldermen (or Councilmen: title varies) *and approved by the Mayor*, 1831–1897 in 65 vols.

By-Laws and Ordinances (revised and printed periodically, e.g. 1845 and 1856).

Manuals of the Corporation of the City of New York, annually 1841/2–1866 ed. David T. Valentine, 1866–1870 and New Series 1916/17–1927 various editors: all known as *Valentine's Manuals* (vols. for 1853, 1869 and 1860 have biographical sketches of mayors and clerks of the city and county).

Alphabetical list of members of the Common Council, etc. (often with the person's occupation, e.g. butcher) 1653–1870, and 12 chronological lists of holders of 12 administrative or judicial positions in the city or county 1626–1871: *Valentine's Manual* for 1870, ed. Hardy, pp. 609–62.

Annual lists of many city, county and port officials, administrative and judicial, including committees, boards and department heads, with residences of aldermen, wards of some officials and office addresses of others: in a special section of the regular N. Y. C. directories starting 1851, and some similar data in appendix of earlier directories.

New York, The World's Metropolis, 1623-4—1923-4, Wm. T. Bonner, 1924 (large number of biographical paragraphs, see especially under government administration).

Oaths and appointments to office, 1834–1924: papers at County Clerk's Office, Hall of Records (cover elected and appointed officials but unindexed before 1865).

Oaths of office of city officials 1833–1835, 1844–1897; oaths and lists of city marshals 1839–1844: now in Municipal Archives and Records Center, 238 William St.

Measurers of grain, lime, lumber and charcoal; city weighers, guagers, wood inspectors, collectors of assessments, street commissioners, justices and clerks, city surveyors, clerks of markets, street inspectors, registers of dogs, etc., 1825–1843: at City Clerk's Office, Municipal Building[47] (a civil list of N. Y. C., names and addresses).

---

[46] Stokes, VI:211.

[47] For prospective transfer of many records of the City Clerk's Office, see note 20.

Municipal Reference Library, Branch of the New York Public Library, Room 2230, Municipal Building, Chambers St.

Municipal Archives and Records Center, Branch of the New York Public Library, Rhinelander Building, 238 William St. (see description earlier in this section of the Guide).

For licensing of lawyers, doctors, and other occupational groups, see the section of this Guide: Name Lists and Biographical Sketches by Occupation.

For state appointments and commissions to many positions in the city, see the following section.

State Civil Appointments and Laws

The state's civil commissions and appointments for the entire state are at Albany. The most convenient summary of state officials is an indexed *Civil List* such as Werner's, but it only gives the more important.

The state issued commissions or appointments to many civil positions in New York County, the following 1821 list [48] being typical with some changes for the period 1783–1846: 4 top administrative posts of the city, 96 positions in the judicial branch, 52 inspectors of produce and manufactures, 7 inspectors of the city's state prison, 3 health officials, 36 port officials and pilots, 1 commissioner of excise, 36 auctioneers, 8 bank directors, 114 public notaries, and 343 commissioners to acknowledge deeds. The state constitution of 1846 transferred to the people of the county the selection of most county and city officers, by election or by appointment through their local officials.

Civil List & Constitutional History of the Colony & State of New York, Edgar A. Werner (index of names in 1883–89 editions, etc.).

1777–1786 Minutes of the Council of Appointment, vol. 1, burned in Fire of 1911; MS index of its civil and military appts. by G. R. Howell is still at NYSL.

1786–1822 Minutes of the Council of Appointment, vols. 2–14 (civil and military), formerly in Secr. of State's Office, now at NYSL.

1770–1822 Records of Commissions, vols. 6–38, formerly at *ibid*. and now at NYSL; abstracts of vols. 6–38 in O'Callaghan Papers at NYHS.

1823–1920 Records of Commissions by the Governor in 12 vols., formerly in Secr. of State's Office, now at NYSL (period of this guide: 1823–1857 in 2 vols.)

1823–1927 Records of Commissions by Governor and Senate in 53 vols., formerly at *ibid*. and now at NYSL (1823–1859 in 7 vols.)

1823–1927 Appointments by Governor and Senate in 41 vols., formerly at *ibid*. and now at NYSL (1823–1859 in 7 vols.)

1804–1878 Abstracts of civil appointments in 6 vols., formerly at *ibid*. and now at NYSL.

The special and private laws of the state generally concern specific organizations and people. Those for organizations (such as churches, civic societies, banks, insurance and business companies) deal with incorporation, altering the name, relief if insolvent, authorization to hold real estate, etc. Those for individuals often concern name changes, aliens (see the Name Changes and Natu-

---

[48] For detailed list, see Study of the Council of Appointment in New York State 1777–1801, Gunther Pohl, MS Master's thesis in New York University library, as taken from *N. Y. Statesman* (Albany newspaper), Oct. 16, 1821 issue.

ralization sections of this Guide) and private claims. An alphabetical list of names with the date is given under private claims on pp. 501–79 of H. H. Havens' *General Index to the Laws of the State of New York 1777–1857*. The majority of private acts for individuals deal with land titles, perhaps a grant to a soldier, more often for the relief (benefit) of heirs, owners, or creditors because of problems arising from alienism (non-citizenship) of some party, from intestacy, minors, etc. Such laws often name the widow (perhaps remarried), minor and adult children, married daughters and their husbands, or sometimes other relatives. Different indexes to the laws will be helpful with different problems because of their varying arrangement; all omit an occasional law as well as names.[49]

General Index to the Laws of the State of New York from 1777 to . . ., printed 1842, 1850, 1859, 1866 and 1902 (unfortunately they index the incomplete compilations before 1802).

Official Index to the Unconsolidated Laws . . . 1778–1919 (1920) (poor for names before 1802).

Laws of the State of New York . . . 1777–1801, repub. in 5 vols., Weed Parsons & Co., 1886–87 at NYHS (complete and indexed; available contemporary editions of this early period were selective).

The Statutory record of the Unconsolidated Laws: being the special, private and local statutes of the State of New York . . . 1778–1911, A. J. Rodenbeck, 2 vols., 1911 at NYPL.

Laws of the State of New York relating particularly to the City of New-York, Gould & Banks, 1833 at NYHS; *Ibid.*, Hy. E. Davies, 1855 at NYPL.

Journal of the Assembly of the State of New-York; Ibid. of the Senate; printed annually, as were the Laws.

Microfilming of legislative, judicial and executive records of all 48 states, territories and colonial possessions has just been completed under a joint project of the Library of Congress and the University of North Carolina, and positive copies of any reel can be purchased. A guide to the contents can be obtained from the Library of Congress for $5. See review in *North Carolina Historical Review*, 28:112, for 1951.

FEDERAL RECORDS

The federal records of this period with which a genealogist is most likely to be concerned are the census records, military records, and passenger lists already discussed in those sections of this Guide. The following publications may also be of use:

American State Papers: Documents Legislative and Executive of the Congress of the United States . . . 1789–1825, ed. Lowrie & Franklin in 38 vols., pub. Gales & Seaton 1834. See especially *Class VI Naval Affairs* (includes lists of navy and marine officers and petty officers with birthplace); *Class IX Claims* (good name index; includes reports on Revolutionary War invalid pensioners examined 1792–95 by judges of the Circuit Court of the U. S. for the Districts of New York, etc.).

---

[49] Thus, the basic adoption law of 1873 is not in the *General Index of 1902*. Thus also, the 1810 act for relief of Mary Kittle otherwise called Mary Fontaine is indexed that year under Kittle, in the *General Index of 1842* under Fontine, and in the *Unconsolidated Laws Index of 1920* under Lansing (it concerns land granted for war services to the deceased soldier Arent Vedder natural son of said Mary, and regranted by this act to her son Alexander Lansing, Jr., and her sons-in-law for her benefit).

*Digested Summary and Alphabetical List of Private Claims which have been pre-
sented to the House of Representatives . . . 1789–1851*, in 3 vols., 1853 (largely
claims of various kinds connected with the Revolution or War of 1812;
claims for pension here listed as tabled or rejected often qualified later under
some broader law if applicant was still living).
Biographical Directory of the American Congress 1774–1949 (1950).

BIRTHS, MARRIAGES, AND DIVORCES

Unfortunately, the state government did not continue the British
system of marriage licenses issued by the Prerogative Court of the
province of New York.

The city's birth and marriage records (as distinguished from such
data in church records) for this period are not useful enough to
warrant a separate section in this Guide. The effective law for
their registration in the city came in force July 1, 1853 (Chap. 75).
The Department of Health also has some earlier registrations for
about 1½ years under an 1847 law and for other reasons. There
are separate libers and alphabetical card indexes for delayed registration of births and marriages (earliest date of either unstated)
and also a small chronological card index of marriages performed
in the Mayor's Office 1855–1888. The overall result is that at
the Department of Health[50] are births as early as 1842 and marriages
as early as 1829, but they are very scanty before 1853 and none too
full until the twentieth century.

Marriages performed by the various mayors and aldermen of New York City,
as well as justices of the peace, etc., 1830–1854, being abstracts of records
at N. Y. County Clerk's Office, MS by Ray C. Sawyer, 1935, at NYPL and
NYHS (includes some marriages by ministers of N. Y. C. churches).

Marriage records 1829–1854 plus handful to 1880, card indexed: at New York
County Clerk's Office[51] (a small group of records).

Marriages performed at the Mayor's Office 1858–1860, 1875–1897, and by Judge
Ehrlich 1886–1895:[52] among the Mayor's Office papers now in Municipal
Archives and Records Center, 238 William St.

For various records of birth and marriage as well as death, see
also the following sections of this Guide: Church Records, Marriage
Notices, Death Notices, Death Records, Burial Records and
Cemeteries.

Divorces were few for the period of this Guide and I have not
examined the subject or the records. But it may be helpful to
summarize the state law of 1787 (Chap. 69) allowing divorces for
adultery. This law provided that the injured party should petition
the chancellor in chancery and he may proceed by sentence or decree in the same court[53] to pronounce the marriage dissolved, but

---

[50] Records of the Dep't of Health, 125 Worth St., New York, N. Y., are not open to the public.
Its indexes of regular series are: births from 1842, marriages from 1829 but mostly unindexed
until 1866, brides from 1866, deaths from 1868.

[51] These form many but not all of the earlier cards in the Dep't of Health's card index of grooms
(for 1829–43, 1846–52, 1865), of the two ꞏꞏꞏꞏꞏꞏꞏꞏꞏ of marriages 1829–46 and 1850–52 in modern
handwriting pinned to the Dep't of Hꞏꞏꞏꞏ Mꞏꞏꞏꞏ ꞏ Registers No. 1 (June 1847–Jany. 1849)
and No. 2 (starting July 1, 1853), and of the occasional insertions in modern handwriting of marriages at their appropriate chronological places in these two libers.

[52] See Stokes, VI: 190 for details; records then at Municipal Reference Library.

[53] For court of chancery records, see Courts in this section and the Probate and Related Records
section

this was in no wise to affect the legitimacy of the children; the chancellor shall take such order for care and maintenance of the children if any and of the wife or any allowance to be made to her as may be proper and sufficient; it shall not be lawful for the party convicted of adultery to remarry but the other party may marry. See also the Revised Statutes of 1813 (Chap. 102) and of 1829 (Chap. 8). The chancellor (and vice chancellor) continued in authority until 1847 when superseded by the Supreme Court. At the New York County Clerk's Office in the Hall of Records are a card index of divorces (confidential) from 1847 on, and the records of several courts having jurisdiction.

NAME CHANGES AND ADOPTIONS

Prior to 1847 an individual formally changed his name by special act of the state legislature: the first or last name might be changed thus, and the reason therefor is often given in the law or the legislative journal.[54] The state law of 1847 (Chap. 464) permitted a New York City resident to apply to any justice of the Supreme Court resident there or to any justice of the Superior Court or judge of the court of common pleas of the county for an order to assume another name, such order to be issued only if the justice is satisfied that the applicant will derive *pecuniary benefit* from assuming another name; documents to be filed in the county clerk's office. The state law of 1860 (Chap. 80) broadened the basis by permitting the court to issue the order if satisfied that there is no reasonable objection to such person assuming another name; a resident of New York City is to apply to the court of common pleas of the county and if a minor to apply by guardian or next friend; returns of such name changes are to be made annually to the Secretary of State, and both old and new names are to be published with the Sessions Laws of each year.

For printed lists of name changes, see the *General Index to the Laws* 1777–1857, pp. 433–36 (incomplete before 1813), and *Ibid.*, 1902, pp. 1309–87. At the New York County Clerk's Office in the Hall of Records are card indexes of changes of name by individuals 1847–1934 and by corporations 1818–1920 (index incomplete for early years) in the records of the various courts under its jurisdiction.

Personal Names: An Annotated Bibliography, Elsdon C. Smith, 1952 (reprint from NYPL *Bulletin* for 1950–51, vols. 54–55).

The Colloquial Who's Who; An Attempt to Identify the Many Authors, Writers and Contributors who have used Pen-Names, Initials, etc., 1600–1924, Wm. Abbatt, 1924 (gives birth and death dates and sometimes occupation, etc.).

Adoptions were first regulated by the state act of 1873 (Chap. 830) to legalize the adoption of minor children by adult persons. It stipulated that proceedings are to be before the county judge

---

[54] Thus, the 1829 act (omitted or incorrectly given in all indexes) to change the names of Wm. Jauncey Thorn and James Jauncey Thorn, infant sons of Herman Thorn of N. Y. C., to Wm. Jauncey and James Jauncey; the 1829 *Journal of the Assembly* adding that these infants were near relatives and large heirs of Wm. Jauncey of N. Y., dec'd, whose will expressed desire for them to thus change their names.

and that a child when adopted shall take the name of the adopting person. It also stated that this act is not to affect proof of adoption heretofore made by any method practised in this state, but hereafter adoptions can only be made under this act. Earlier indirect regulation under the 1860 changes of name law has just been mentioned. Presumably proof of adoption heretofore practised[55] refers primarily to direct mention in a will or, failing such, to proofs that might be presented in various courts by individuals claiming right to inherit by adoption. The most likely source would probably be the voluminous and hard-to-use records of various civil courts at the Court of Appeals Office and at the New York County Clerk's Office, or of the Surrogate's Court. At the New York County Clerk's Office are confidential records of adoptions in the Court of Common Pleas, starting 1874, card indexed, and others located through its Miscellaneous card file 1812–1934. Helpful information on a particular situation might be found occasionally in indentures (see next section) and in guardianship records (see previous Probate and Related Records section of this Guide).

The 1887 law (Chap. 703) revised the above 1873 law to include (rather than exclude) right of inheritance for the child so adopted, whose heirs and next of kin are to be the same as if said child was the legitimate child of the adopting person (with one exception).

APPRENTICES AND THE POOR

Indenture was the name given to a previously customary form of contract for services. The purpose varied: to pay for ship passage, to learn a trade, to take care of poor children. A study should be made of the custom of indenturing in New York. All the illustrations here given, from among the indenture papers at NYHS, summarize the information on printed forms duly filled in with particulars.

Many immigrants to America were too poor to pay directly for their passage; they did so by selling their services for a term of years under an indenture.

Indenture Sept. 28, 1807 between Alicia Smith, an emigrant lately from Ireland but now of New York City, and Thomas Davis of New York City, porter vault keeper, that she is aged 28 years and for the $45 he paid for her passage in the Ship Susan, Capt. Collins, from Dublin, Ireland to New York, she binds herself as servant to said Thomas Davis for four years, and she is to get the yearly sum of $18.16 and clothes; signed by Thomas Davis and the mark of Alicia Smith, and acknowledged before a special justice relating to the peace of New York City.

Apprenticeship was the accepted method of learning a trade, so it is not only the poor that we find on such records. The agreement took the form of indenture.

Indenture July 26, 1801 John Countess of New York City aged 14 years, with consent of his guardian Isaac Caldwell, hath put himself apprentice to Alexander

---

[55] An early reference to adoption is in the 1829 *Journal of the Assembly:* Ann Eliza Babcock is an orphan and resides in the family of James Sealy of Albany; said Sealy and his wife are aged and respected people without children and have recently adopted the petitioner and they intend to make her their heir at their death. The 1829 act (Chap. 88) authorized Ann Eliza Babcock of Albany to take the maiden name of Seeley (omitted from Unconsolidated Laws Index).

McLaurin of New York City, mariner, to learn the trade of mariner and navigation, for a term of three years; signed by all three persons concerned.

Indenture Feb. 9, 1807 John Cromwell, Jr., aged 15 years, 3 months & 27 days, with consent of John Cromwell of New York City butcher his father, do apprentice himself to Andrew Wheeler of New York City, butcher, for 5 years, 8 months & 3 days; signed by the two Cromwells, and acknowledged before a special justice relating to the peace of New York City.

The state law of 1788, called an act relating to apprentices and servants, authorized the overseers of the poor of New York City, with the consent of the mayor, etc., to bind out poor children. As this practice was extended to infants far too young to work, it was evidently a method of finding a home for poor children. Indeed, in a few of these indentures, which regularly were apprenticeships, the terms apprentice and master on the form were crossed out and the terms child, parent, and to be adopted were inserted. In the instance here cited, it will be noted that the adoption was for the period of the child's minority only, and Mr. Volens, Chief Clerk of the New York County Clerk's Office, is under the impression that a child did not inherit under such an "adoption".

Indenture Nov. 15, 1792 John Ware, aged 8 years, 9 months and 20 days with consent of his mother Cathn. Hunter, of two Aldermen of N. Y. C. and of the Commissioners of the Almshouse, do apprentice himself to Hugh McConnel of Orange County to learn the trade of a farmer, for 12 years, 2 months and 10 days, and he shall be taught to read, write and cypher through the single rule of 3 and be given clothes; signed by two aldermen and the mark of McConnel.

Feb. 26, 1858 Robert Lennon aged 3 months hath put himself, with approbation of the Governor of the Alms House of New York City [as apprentice: crossed out] to be adopted to Moses Van Vliet & Sarah M. his wife residing at Rhinebeck after the manner of an adopted child to serve 20 years & 9 months, and to be taught agriculture or some other reputable business; signed by Moses Van Vliet.

April 13, 1891 Mary W. Mohrbach aged 3 months, with consent of the Commissioners of Public Charities, do put herself apprentice to John & Mary Waters of 245 Ave B, New York City for 20 years & 9 months to learn housekeeping and plain sewing; signed by both Sadie Heiner as mother of the child and Mary Waters.

The NYHS has 40 volumes and 2 packages of indentures, 1792–1794, 1804–1811,[56] 1805–1891, and 1815–1915, the last two groups being 1 package and 38 volumes of Boys' and Girls' Indentures given by the Department of Welfare in 1937. Not given, perhaps because under a different custodian, are two similar Department of Welfare libers, one of boys and girls bound 1794–1815 and one of boys' indentures 1807–1810.[57] Indentures under the New York County Clerk's jurisdiction are few and early but may be located through its two card indexes of Pleadings (and misc. early papers) and Miscellaneous File.

[56] Some of these indentures (for apprenticeship and passage money) are with the consent and approval of one of the Special Justices for preserving the Peace in N. Y. C. and usually signed by Jacob DelaMontagnie, Special Justice. Inquiry to the County Clerk's Office, City Court, law l ibrarian in the Criminal Courts building and Municipal Reference Library, also Stokes' listing of City Clerk's and Mayor's Office records, have disclosed neither indentures for passage money nor DelaMontagnie's records. No thorough search.

[57] See Stokes, VI:210, and last paragraph of this Guide's note 27.

Other kinds of records on the poor are in many special series under the Department of Welfare of New York City, including: admissions, discharges, and deaths at the Almshouse 1759–1847; nursing children 1819–1845 (giving birthdate and parents); census of inmates 1789–1832; deaths 1804–1834 (giving name and birthplace); and relief of the emigrant poor 1809–1815.[58]

NEWSPAPERS

Newspapers afford a wealth of material for the patient searcher. Of special note are death and marriage notices, obituary sketches that became popular and longer as the century progressed, business advertisements — especially those of importers and merchants, notices of new and terminated partnerships, notices for settling debts or for repudiating a wife's debts, and executors' notices. The best collections of newspapers are at NYPL[59] and at NYHS. See *Checklist of newspapers and official gazettes in The New York Public Library*, D. C. Haskell, 1915. The NYHS's excellent newspaper collection is being rounded out both by photostats of missing rare issues and by acquisition, the most recent for this period being the entire file of the New York Sun, 1833–1950.

Historical Incidents from Newspapers, 1696–1850, Thomas DeVoe, 3 vols., MS at NYHS (events in N. Y. C. from N. Y. and other papers; index to names of persons includes some marriages and deaths).

Checklist of New York City newspapers arranged by the year, 1725–1811, in Stokes' *Iconography*, 2:431–52.

New York City Newspapers 1820–1850, A Bibliography, Louis H. Fox, in *Papers of the Bibliographical Society of America* for 1927, v. 21 (gives the paper's slant — political party, labor, literary, religious, etc.).

History and Bibliography of American Newspapers, 1690–1820, Clarence S. Brigham, 1947.

American Newspapers 1821–1936, a Union List of files available in the U. S. and Canada, Winifred Gregory, 1937.

PHOTOGRAPHS, ACCOUNT BOOKS, MINUTES, FAMILY PAPERS, ETC.

The New-York Historical Society, organized 1804, in addition to sources mentioned throughout this Guide, has much contemporary material including those of little-known and short-lived organizations, such as circulars, proceedings, and minutes. It has numerous account books and letter books of individual firms and the papers of various families, as well as Mrs. Bella C. Landauer's collection of business trade cards, advertisements, etc. It also has a good collection of prints and photographs of many residences and other buildings in the city. Similar statements are applicable to collections at NYPL. The NYPL has a sizable card index of the views of New York City's streets, buildings, etc., appearing in printed books, as well as the famous Phelps Stokes collection of prints of New York City.

---

[58] See Stokes, VI:209–10. I have not used these Dep't of Welfare records and cannot comment on their present availability or usefulness to the genealogist.

[59] The newspaper division of NYPL is at 137 West 25th St., open to those who obtain a pass at the administration office in the main library on 42nd St.

But some files are in special rooms of the main library.

For portraits, photographs and prints of people, see Guides to Portraits and Pohl's index both in my Secondary Sources section, also various books throughout the section of this Guide: Name Lists and Biographical Sketches by Occupation.

CHURCH RECORDS

The multiplication of churches as New York City expanded — from 22 in 1789, to 101 in 1827, to 150 in 1837, and so forth[60] — renders the problem of the genealogist very difficult, doubly so since very few church records of the nineteenth century are available in libraries so that the searcher must usually go to the church. This poses the problem of identifying the church by its present name and of having some advance idea of what vital records might be available, since many churches are not equipped to answer inquiries (let alone make searches) and some do not know the contents of their early records.

The following table of about 60 churches in existence 1783–1814 supplies the researcher with some answers. Its genesis was my study of the churches named in the cemetery column of the city's Death Register No. 1 (1801–1814). I increased their number about 60% by study of contemporary sources: city directories, guides to the city, city maps, street identifications. It is quite possible that I missed some churches existing for only a few years, especially those without church edifices, and that I have incorrectly classified one or two of the evanescent independent churches found. The information thus obtained I have amplified and brought up-to-date to the extent feasible for a summary of this sort by study of Stokes' *Iconography*, Greenleaf's and Disosway's histories of early New York City churches and histories of individual churches and denominations, and by correspondence with about fifteen churches. The various early negro churches have been omitted because their lack of early records made it pointless to disentangle the many discrepancies concerning their history.

In using this table, its purpose should be borne in mind. It is not intended to be a definitive study, and the manner in which it was compiled involves minor errors. The searcher wishing authoritative information on a particular church must arrange to study that church's records.

This table is designed as an aid to the genealogical researcher, primarily in guiding him to desired church records. The first column is devoted to a church's names and existence, the second column to its location over a period centered in the early 1800's, and the third column to the existence and location of its vital records. Listing of popular and official names of a church will aid the searcher in recognizing it despite variable references on records as well as secondary material; he should note that a few churches, even of different denominations, were known by the

[60] *The City of New York in . . . 1789*, Thomas E. V. Smith, 1889, p. 125; *Description of the City of New-York*, James Hardie, 1827; *New-York as it is, in 1837*, pr. J. Disturnell, 1837.

same or confusingly similar names. The searcher will often use the church location column in conjunction with directories, maps, and land records. Study of addresses is sometimes needed to identify the church of the minister who officiated at a marriage or funeral noted in a newspaper (see the section: Means of Identifying the Church of a Minister). The searcher may not have even this clue to a family's church, but it is a good bet that because of the poor transportation facilities of the period, his home and his church were in the same locality of the city. Hence, this column will be helpful (when the denomination can be assumed) in narrowing to several the field of possible churches in which a family might be baptized and married. Conversely, when a family's church is known or can be assumed, use of directories and other records can be speeded by being able to disregard other people of the same name who lived too far from that church. The organization date of a church not only indicates when various records may have been started but also may help the searcher in deciding whether to turn to another church's records if this church's existing records do not start early enough. Complete series of records for the latter part of this period will be so voluminous that (unless the churches have indexed them) a genealogist cannot — for most searches — cover all vital records in one of the larger denominations; hence, if a man is known to have gone to a well-established church whose early records do not exist and if his earlier addresses were near that church's early locations, the genealogist may do better as a rule to concentrate on other than church records.

Old	New	Old	New
Amos	—West 10th	Garden	—Exchange Place
Anthony	—Worth	Hamilton Square	—at 69th St. and Lexington Ave.
Barley	—part of Duane		
Bloomingdale	—approx. Broadway above 14th St.	Herring	—part of Bleecker
		Magazine	—Pearl near Broadway
Budd	—Van Dam	Mill	—South William
Bullock	—Broome	Nicholas	—Walker
Chapel	—West Broadway	Nicholas Wm.	—near Astor Place
Cross	—Park St.	North	—East Houston
Elm	—Lafayette	Orange	—Baxter
Fair	—Fulton St. east of Broadway	Partition	—Fulton west of Broadway
		Pump	—part of Canal
Fayette	—Oliver	Second	—Forsyth
First	—Chrystie	Sugar Loaf	—part of Franklin
Fourth	—Allen	Walker	—Canal east of Baxter

Note to third column. The third column is based on the information printed in the W.P.A. *Guide to Vital Statistics in the City of New York: Borough of Manhattan—Churches,* 1942. This is a good compilation, so I have not verified such records in possession of churches, having communicated with only about fifteen churches whose records seemed lacking and especially important. I have corrected a few errors and I have verified and brought up-to-date its listings of records in the chief religious depositories, finding that many are now elsewhere. My chief contributions to this column are including records of early churches not covered by the W.P.A. Guide and listing those church vital records that are printed or available at the main research libraries, through examination of their collections.

The date listed is the date on which existing baptismal and/or marriage records start. Occasionally some of the less important kind of records are mentioned in parenthesis. Records are believed in possession of the church, unless stated otherwise. Lack of dates in the column indicates that vital records have not been located. Occasionally a little-known church is identified by its minister's name. In many denominations, only one series of records was kept until the early 1800's, whether the relationship between its churches was called united, collegiate, society of, or chapels of. Only a few churches have continued this relationship to the present day.

The following is a key to the abbreviations in the last column:

m	manuscript collections of (copies or abstracts, written or typed)	H	The New-York Historical Society
o	original records	HS	The Holland Society
ph	photostat copies	LI	Long Island Historical Society
p	publications of (such as quarterly, yearbook, or printed collections)	NB	Gardner Sage Library, Theological Seminary, New Brunswick, N. J.
G	N. Y. Genealogical and Biographical Society	PB	N. Y. Presbytery, 156 Fifth Ave.
		PL	N. Y. Public Library, 42nd St.
		SL	State Library, Albany, N. Y.

CHURCHES IN EXISTENCE 1783–1814

Denomination and Church Names of Church and Cemetery Period of Church Existence	Location of Church in the early 1800's Years Streets		Church's Existing Vital Records Location 1952 if away from church Date begin Copies & Originals
Baptist[81]			
First Baptist**	o1762–1840	Gold St., John	1788 mar; perhaps 1762 for bp, memb, & d: in deacons & trustees minutes
Oliver St. Church† Fayette St. Church 2nd Baptist Epiphany Church dissolved 1908	o1770 and split o1791–1862	Fayette,* Henry	(1835 funerals) Ho no other V.R. at H (despite WPA). Some of its records (kind & period unstated) at Calvary Baptist Church
Bethel Baptist 2nd and 3rd Baptist dissolved 1840	o1770 and split o1791–1806 1806–1819	Rose St. Broome St.	
Fair St. Baptist† Church of Christ dissolved 1801	o1795–1801	Fair St.*	1794–1830 mar by Rev. Jn Stanford, also chaplain of prison and charitable houses Hp(v.21) Ho
Ebenezer Baptist† Scotch Baptists split 1810 to Disciples of Christ	o1805–1811c c1812–	Anthony* York	Another Ebenezer Church org. 1825, dissolved 1849
Welsh Baptist† dissolved 1813	o1807–1813	Mott St., Walker	
Mulberry St. Baptist dissolved 1839	o1809–1839	Mulberry, Chatham	Records lost c50 yrs ago *per* pastor of successor Tabernacle Church Membership list not at Baptist City Society (despite WPA)
North Baptist† Beriah Baptist merged c1890 into North Church (o1827)**	o1809–1819 1820–1865c	Budd,* Varick MacDougal	
Independent† formerly Universalist	1807–1808	Rose, Pearl	Rev. A. McClay (minister 1809 of Mulberry St. Baptist Church)
Zoar Baptist† dissolved 1812	1811–1812	Rose, Pearl	Rev. M. Earle
Catholic			
St. Peter's**	o1785–now	Barclay St., Church	1787 U.S. Cath. Hist. Soc: *Records*, v.3
St. Patrick's†**	o1809–now	Mott St.	1820. Earlier rec. with St. Peter's

[81] Inquiries to the Baptist City Society, to Samuel Colgate Baptist Hist. Coll. at Rochester, N. Y., and to Amer. Baptist Hist. Soc. at Chester, Pa. (no reply from last) have not resulted in locating records of these churches. The pastor of Calvary Baptist Church wrote me that Baptist churches do not maintain complete bapt. or mar. records as they are not concerned with the ancestry of the individual (adult) when he is bapt. and as marriage records are the property of the minister. Some of the latter have found their way into collections, e.g. Marriages 1834–85 by Rev. Wm. Williams of Amity St. Baptist Church at NYHS.

Denomination and Church Names of Church and Cemetery Period of Church Existence	Location of Church in the early 1800's Years	Streets	Church's Existing Vital Records Location 1952 if away from church Date begin Copies and Originals
Congregational			
Independent† dissolved c1820	1789–1820c	Broadway, Anthony*	Rev. George Wall
First Congregational† Presbyterian 1811–13 dissolved 1816	1803–1811 1813–1816	Warren St. Elizabeth St.	Rev. John Townley
Disciples of Christ			
Church of Christ Sandemanian Scotch Baptist now: Park Ave. Christian	o1810–	by 1831 at York St.	Hy Errett elected Elder 1816 1850. (early membership rolls)
Episcopal			
Trinity**	o1697–now	Broadway & Rector	1746 Gmp (v. 67, v. 69) 1812 mar Bishop Onderdonk Ho (1711 & 1736 subscr: Berrian's *History*) (burials 1777) Gm
St. George's**† Trinity chapel to 1811	1750–1841	Beekman, Cliff	1809 Rec. as chapel with Trinity's
St. Paul's** chapel of Trinity	1764–now	Broadway & Partition*	1809 Gm Earlier rec. with Trinity's
Christ's**	o1793–1823	Ann St., William	1793 Gmp(v.42) Hm SLm
St. Mark's**	o1795–now	Stuyvesant	1799 Gmp(v.71) (1799 pewholders: *Memorial* pr. 1899)
St. Stephen's**	o1805–1866	First St.* & Bullock*	1809 (1805 subscr: *History* pr.1906)
St. John's chapel of Trinity merged 1909 into: St. Lukes Chapel	1803–1909	Varick, Laight	1834 Earlier rec. with Trinity's
St. Michael's**†	o1807–1853	Bloomingdale* (Bwy at 99th St.)	1808 (1807 pewholders: *History* pr. 1907)
Grace**†	o1808–1845	Broadway & Rector	1809
St. James**†	o1810–1869	Hamilton Sq.*	1810
St. Esprit** The French Church Reformed before 1804	1804–1831	Pine, Nassau	1804 Hph
Zion Eng. Lutheran before 1810 merged 1890 and 1922: now St. Matthew & St. Timothy	1810–1815 1818–1853	Mott, Pearl Mott & Cross*	1810 Ho
Jewish			
Hebrews (o1655) Congregation Shearith Israel**	1728–1833	Mill St.,* Broad	1759. (1699 inscriptions, New Bowery Cem.; 1728 contrib; 1790 memb; 1804 mar: *Amer. Jew. Hist.*, v.18, v.21, v.27) *Portraits etched in Stone*, Pool
Lutheran			
German Lutheran (o1664) The Swamp Church United German (Trinity and Christ) Lutheran now: St. Matthew's Luth.	1767–1831	William & Frankfort	1704 Trinity Gm HSp(1903) 1752 Christ Gmp(v.73) 1827 St. Matthew's Ho
English Lutheran Zion Episcopal after 1810	1797–1801 1802–1810	Magazine St.* Mott, Pearl	1794 Ho
Methodist[62]			
Methodist Church and Society in the City of New York: combined name for the churches below			One set of early records for all its churches in the city (earliest called John St. Church records) 1799 mar. (1811 memb.) PLo
Methodist's Wesley Chapel now: John St. Methodist	o1766–now	John St., Dutch St.	1785 PLph Gm Meth. Hist. Soc. (1768 subscr.) PLph Meth. Hist. Soc. 1796 and 1820 Gm. 1796 PLo

[62] These churches were Methodist Episcopal, although the term was seldom used before the split in 1830 into Methodist Episcopal and Methodist Protestant.

Denomination and Church Names of Church and Cemetery Period of Church Existence	Location of Church in the early 1800's Years Streets	Church's Existing Vital Records Location 1952 if away from church Date begin Copies and Originals
Forsyth St. Methodist† Second St. Methodist Bowery Methodist 2nd Methodist dissolved 1904	o1789–1904 Second St.,* Division	1837 (1822 classes) PLo 1837 Gm
Duane St. Methodist North Methodist Hudson Methodist 3rd Methodist merged 1939 into: Metropolitan Temple	o1797–1863 Duane St., Greenwich	1810 Gm PLo 1838 (1794 memb) Metrop. Temple 1838 Gm
Bowery Village Church† Two Mile Stone Church Seventh St. Methodist dissolved 1911	o1800–1837 Nicholas Wm.*	1837 Gm (1833 classes) PLo
Greenwich (Village) Church† Bedford St. Church merged 1913 into: Metropolitan Temple	o1807–1913 Bedford St., Morton	1838 Gm Metrop. Temple
Allen St. Church Fourth St. Methodist dissolved 1902	o1810–1836 Fourth St.,* Delancey	1811 Gm PLo
Moravian United Brethren Moravians now: First Moravian	o1749–1844 Fair St.,* William	1744 Gm Hph
Presbyterian Presbyterian organization United Presbyterians		Collegiate body to 1809: its records are part of 1st Presb. Church's. 1804 Hp(v.2) Ho
1st Presbyterian** collegiate to 1809	o1716–1844 Wall St., Broadway	1728 (deaths 1786) Gmp(v.4;v.11) 1804 Hp(v.2) Ho
Brick Presbyterian** New or 2nd Presbyterian collegiate to 1809	1767–1856 Beekman & Nassau & the Park	1809–1908 printed by the church, Earlier rec. with 1st Presb.'s (1768 inscriptions) Gp(v.60)
Rutgers St. Presbyterian collegiate to 1809 now: Rutgers Presb.	1798–1863 Rutgers St. & Henry	1809 Earlier rec. with 1st Presb.'s
Cedar St. Presbyterian† now: Fifth Ave. Presb.	o1808–1835 Cedar, William	1808 (1808 memb: *History*, pr. 1908)
Irish Presbyterian Orange St. Presbyterian Canal St. Presbyterian Greene St. Church dissolved 1894	o1808–1825 Orange St.,* Grand	1815–1831 bap, 1816–1853 mar Go
Spring St. Presbyterian**† (split 1826 into Laight St. Presb. Ch; dissolved 1843)	o1811–now Spring St., Varick	1811 in N.J. home of Clerk of the Session: Gustave C. Indruk, c/o Tappen & Indruk Co, 260 W. Bwy, N.Y.C. 1811 Laight St. Church set PBo
Elizabeth St. Presbyterian† Congregational after 1813	1811–1813 Elizabeth, Hester	
Scotch Church on Cedar St. Scots' Presbyterian 1st Associate Reformed now: 2nd Presbyterian	o1756–1836 Cedar St., Broadway	1844 (1784 minutes; 1786 pew list) at church (1785–98 pew rents, burials) Ho
2nd Associate Reformed Pearl St. Church New Scots' Presbyterian merged 1853 into: Central Presbyterian	1797–1853 Magazine,* Elm*	1805 (1804 memb.) Earlier rec. with Scotch Church on Cedar St.'s rec., as collegiate with it to 1804
3rd Associate Reformed Murray St. Church Eighth St. Church dissolved 1852	o1810–1841 Murray St.	1812 PBo (1823–48 vaults and pew rents) Ho *Catalogue of Officers and Members, 1830* PL
1st Associate Seceders Meeting House Cameronians Associate Scotch Presb. Grand St. Presb. now: 4th Presbyterian	o1785–1824 Nassau, John‡	1802 bap.; 1821 mar. (1851 deaths; 1795 minutes) (merged 1953, moving as 4th Presb. to The Bronx)

63

Denomination and Church Names of Church and Cemetery Period of Church Existence	Location of Church in the early 1800's Years	Streets	Church's Existing Vital Records Location 1952 if away from church Date begin Copies and Originals
Reformed Presbyterian Reformed Scots Associate Covenanters merged 1907 into: 2nd Presbyterian	o1797–1835	Chambers, Broadway	(1797 memb.; minutes "complete")
Quaker Friends** (o1671c) Old Meeting House New Meeting House Separation 1828 into Orthodox & Hicksite branches	1747–1826 1776–1824	Liberty St. Pearl, Oak	Records of both branches at 15th St. Meeting House 1640 old Flushing Mo. Mtg. rec. also in Gmp(v.3,6,7) LIm Hm Hinshaw's *Encyclopedia*, v.III 1771 N.Y.C. Mo. Mtg. rec. also at Gm LIm (1796 burials) LIm
Reformed Collegiate Church** (o1628) collegiate body still exists, churches in it changing			Records of the churches of the Collegiate Church at 45 John St. 1639 Gmp(v.5,6,70,59) (1727 burials) Gmp(v.75) HS(1899)
South Dutch collegiate to 1812 dissolved 1918	1693–1835	Garden St.*	1812 Gm SLm (1839 memb) NBo Earlier rec. with Collegiate's
Middle Dutch New Dutch dissolved 1844	1729–1844	Nassau & Cedar	Records a part of above Collegiate Church's
North Dutch dissolved 1875	1769–1875	William & Fulton	Records a part of above Collegiate Church's
Greenwich Dutch New Dutch NorthWest Reformed (1819 split to 8th Presb.) dissolved c1866	o1803–1827 1827–1864	Amos & Chas. Amos* & Herring*	1806 bap.; 1808 mar. Gm Hm SLm NBo (1804 memb.; 1859 deaths) NBo
Bloomingdale Dutch† Church of Harsenville dissolved 1913	o1805–1869	Bloomingdale* (Bwy & 69–68th Sts.)	1808 Mott's *N.Y. of Yesterday: Bloomingdale*, 1908 NBo
Northwest Dutch Franklin St. Church New Dutch Madison Ave. Reformed dissolved c1918	o1808–1854	Sugar Loaf* Chapel*	1808 Gm SLm NBo
Harlem Dutch† now: Elmendorf Chapel	1768–1825	Harlem (1st Ave. & 125th)	1806 Gmp(v.8) (1672–94 deacons records in Dutch, Riker Coll at PL)
French Protestant (o1688) French Huguenot Church after 1804 Episcopal	1704–1804	Pine St., Nassau	1688 *Collec. of Huguenot Soc. of N.Y.*,v.1 (1866) Hph
German Reformed** German Calvinist Reformed Calvinist	o1758–1822	Nassau, Maiden Lane	1758 Ho 1805 at the church, 351 E.68
Universalist Universalists United Christian Friends	o1796–1801 1801–1818 1818–1837	Vandewater Magazine* Duane	1808–34 mar. by Edw. Mitchell Ho (1796 memb.; 1801 and 1819 pew rents) Ho
Independent† Universalist	c1805–		Rev. John Foster

The churches after 1814 become too numerous to include in a general guide of this sort. However, I feel I should mention three religious movements established in New York City shortly after 1814, here summarized in the same manner as the foregoing table: —

Swedenborgian Church of the New Jerusalem New Church now: N.Y. Society of New Church	o1816– 1821–	Broadway Pearl, Cross*	1839
Unitarian Unitarian Church of Divine Unity now: All Souls Unitarian	o1819–	Chambers St., Church St.	1819 (org. 1819 as Unitarian Society and incorp. 1819 as First Congregational Church of N.Y.)
Undenominational Mariners Church	1819–	Roosevelt St.	1822 Rev. Hy Chase Gm Ho

The searcher who needs records of later nineteenth century churches, existing or defunct, might (1) consult the W.P.A. guides, (2) use references listed in the Means of Identifying the Church of an Officiating Minister section of this Guide; (3) study directories, maps and descriptive accounts of the city, contemporary with the period he is interested in, and (4) make inquiries to various religious headquarters, if the desired records are not at NYHS and NYPL. (The latter has almost all Methodist records.) A short suggestive list follows:

Guide to Vital Statistics in the City of New York: Borough of Manhattan — Churches, Work Projects Administration, 1942.

Inventory of the Church Archives in New York City, Work Projects Administration (set never finished) volumes available on: Roman Catholic, Eastern Orthodox, Protestant Episcopal, Lutheran, Methodist Church (Meth. Episcopal), Presbyterian Church in U. S. A., Quaker, Reformed Church in America (Dutch, French and German); has for each sect an alphabetical list of the first and current ministers of its churches.[63]

The Picture of New-York, and Stranger's Guide, A. T. Goodrich, 1828.

1836 map of the city, in Stokes' *Iconography,* III: plate 99.

Doggett's *New-York City and Co-Partnership Directory for 1843 & 1844.*

1851 and 1867 plans of the city, pub. Mathew Dripps.

Rise of the Jewish Community of New York, 1654–1860, Hyman B. Grinstein, 1945.

Baptist: Baptist City Society, 152 Madison Ave., New York, N. Y.

Catholic: Chancery of the Archdiocese of New York, 451 Madison Ave., New York, N. Y.

Episcopal: Rev. Lawrence B. Larsen, Registrar of Diocese of New York (successor to Rev. Floyd Van Keuren listed in W. P. A. Guide), 1047 Amsterdam Ave., New York, N. Y.
Rev. H. Rushton Bell, Director of Chaplaincy, N. Y. Prot. Episcopal City Mission Society, 38 Bleecker St., New York, N. Y.

Methodist Episcopal: Manuscript Room, New York Public Library, 42nd St., New York, N. Y.
Methodist Historical Society Library, 150 Fifth Ave., New York, N. Y.

Presbyterian: New York Presbytery Office, 156 Fifth Ave., New York, N. Y.

Quaker: Mr. Percy Clapp, Keeper of the Records, Friends Meeting House, 221 East 15th St., New York, N. Y. (for Friends records for the entire state of New York).

Reformed Dutch: Gardner Sage Library, Theological Seminary, New Brunswick, N. J. For the Collegiate churches: Mr. Walter C. Herrod, Clerk, Collegiate Corporation office, 45 John St., New York, N. Y.

---

[63] These are handy lists and might well have been included in the section Means of Identifying the Church of a Minister.

GUIDE TO GENEALOGICAL AND BIOGRAPHICAL SOURCES FOR NEW YORK CITY

SUPPLEMENT 1855–1898 WITH ADDENDA 1783–1855

By ROSALIE FELLOWS BAILEY, of New York City
Fellow of The American Society of Genealogists

This is a guide to the old kinds of sources for old New York City (Manhattan),[64] hence the ending date 1898 has been chosen in order to include the Spanish-American War and exclude the outlying boroughs of the present Greater New York City, created 1 Jan. 1898 by charter of 1897.

Genealogical and biographical research in the second half of the nineteenth century is far easier and has an entirely different approach from the previous three-quarter century. While such a statement probably applies to most of the United States, it may be stated with special emphasis for New York City, which has increasingly full death records and obituaries for the later period, as well as lists of next of kin in the probate records. Through biographical and family data contained therein (and family knowledge), the desired person may be identified and others of the same name discarded, and there will usually be numerous clues by which to identify the previous generation and previous geographical location of the family. Hence for this later period, there is seldom the problem of gathering sufficient leads with which to start ancestral search, which is so difficult for the post-revolutionary half century. The difficulty for the late nineteenth century is more likely to be the carrying forward of various branches of a family, especially if they moved out of town and are unknown to the branch with which the searcher has contact. This problem may be ignored in genealogies by not continuing such branches, but it must be dealt with in the settlement of estates (usually intestate) that are to be divided among distant kin.

As this is a Guide rather than a Bibliography,[65] the far easier late nineteenth century period will not be covered here as minutely

---

[64] This Guide does not discuss the 1895 change in the court system nor sources for The Bronx, parts of which were taken from Westchester County and added to New York County in 1874 and 1895.

[65] Surprise having been expressed that in some instances I have included the name of a special library in a list of specific sources on a subject, I want to emphasize again that this is not a bibliography but a guide. I myself find it most useful to know that there is a special place to go to for a certain subject.

as was the post-revolutionary period. Seldom would a searcher have need for small little-known lists. Moreover, the original source material is better known and more likely to be available. The groundwork and sometimes the late-period details have been covered in the main portion of this Guide.

Three new sections have been added: Birth, Marriage, and Death Indexes; Voting; and Removals from New York City; also a subsection of Biographical Compendiums. Otherwise this Supplement has been set up with the same sections and arrangement[66] as the main Guide to facilitate their combined use. An index is planned for the reprint.

The term "manuscript" has been used throughout in the sense of "unprinted compilation". At the present time, most manuscripts cited in this Guide (e.g. abstracts or copies of church records, of wills, and of newspaper notices) are kept in the manuscript room or section of the NYGB and NYSL, and in the genealogical divisions of the NYPL and NYHS. The titles of printed works are in italics, and titles of original records are in regular type.

PROBATE AND RELATED RECORDS

Annual Reports of the Public Administrator for 1839 through 1871, printed annually in *Documents of the Board of Aldermen of the City of New York*, 1839–40 to 1872: reports for 1839–1853 give name, occupation, "residence or where from", and amounts, for new estates and those already reported; reports for 1854–1871 give also date of letters of administration (oldest listed, 1824), residence at death (i.e. death place), and "country from which he came if not a resident of the state at death" (this column almost always lists a nation or a state of the U. S.). Public Administrator reports were also sometimes printed in a newspaper, e.g., *N. Y. Daily News* of Jan. 28, 1856, *N. Y. Daily Transcript* of Jan. 15, 1863, and of Feb. 12, 1866.

DEATH NOTICES

Early American periodicals report a surprising number of marriages and deaths, but such notices need to be abstracted to be useful to the average searcher. Death notices are also to be found in almanacs. For checklists of both, see the Secondary Sources section of the Supplement.

"Old New York and Trinity Church", in NYHS *Collections* for 1870, pp. 145–408 (newspaper notices 1730–1790 mentioning the church or its ministers, hence marriage and death notices).

DEATH RECORDS

Death records of the city's Department of Health become progressively fuller toward the end of the century; they give length of time resident in the city, parents' birthplaces starting January 1867, and parents' names starting September 1881, etc. For indexes, see the section below.

If the cemetery's name is incompletely entered on the death record (e.g. as Cypress Hills, where there are about a dozen cemeteries), it may be identifiable in records of the undertaker located

---

[66] Exception: placing of the Birth, Marriage, and Divorce Records section.

through the telephone book or through either the Metropolitan Funeral Directors Association, Inc., N.Y.C., or Chief of Funeral Directing, Department of Health, Albany, N. Y.

Sporadic cases of yellow fever also occurred in this city in the years 1794, 1796, 1797, 1800, 1801, and 1802; for these and for the slight epidemics of 1793, 1799, and 1803, refer to death notices in newspapers and the city's fragmentary death records. An additional source for 1795 is:

List of Patients under Medical Care for the Epidemical Yellow Fever, in Belle-Vue Hospital, 1795, Dr. Alexander Anderson, at NYHS (see NYHS *Quarterly*, 37:221).

Death records, 1801–1866, previously described, include columns for the sexton and the cemetery, the latter usually being entered with the name of the church.

See also the following sections of this Guide: Church records, Death notices, Burial records and cemeteries.

BIRTH, MARRIAGE, AND DIVORCE RECORDS

The scarcity of official records of births, marriages, and divorces for the 1783–1855 period led to relegating mention of them to the end of the main Guide (under this subhead in the Special Records section). Since the discussion thereon largely concerns post-1855 records, it was included primarily to forestall queries on the existence of early records, but if a supplement had then been contemplated for the later period, it would have been postponed for more appropriate entry in the supplement near the Death Records section. My apologies are extended to the searcher for this arrangement, the inconvenience of which will be lessened by the index in the reprint.

Marriage records of the City's Department of Health give considerable data, including names of both parents of both bride and groom starting 1867.

BIRTH, MARRIAGE, AND DEATH INDEXES

The inquirer should not be surprised if the Department of Health fails to locate a desired vital record of a date earlier than its indexes: a record might not have been filed or, if filed, it might have been missed among the voluminous, chronological, handwritten, and sometimes obscure entries of the early period. It is therefore helpful to know the coverage of the indexes.

The indexes of births, marriages and deaths previously given in note 50 are the Department of Health's card indexes, not open to the public. The Department also has printed indexes of births, marriages (grooms), and deaths, starting with such records for August 1888, printed annually, of which only the marriage index is open to the public and is at NYPL.

MEANS OF IDENTIFYING THE CHURCH OF AN OFFICIATING MINISTER

With the items listed below, the ministers of the city's Lutheran churches are as readily identifiable, and those of the Catholic and

Episcopal churches almost so, as those of the Dutch, Jewish, and Presbyterian churches previously cited in this section of the Guide.

Geschichte des Evangelisch-Lutherischen Ministeriums vom Staats New York, John Nicum, 1888 (has a list of the 380 Lutheran ministers in the state from before 1792 to 1888 with death date and place, etc.; list of Lutheran churches each with its ministers, secretary, and treasurer).

Sadlier's Catholic Directory (variant early names including *Metropolitan Catholic Almanac and Laity's Directory* for 1838–1860), 1822 at Archdiocese' office, from 1835 almost annually at NYPL (lists of Catholic churches by diocese, town, church name and address, with clergy of each; alphabetical lists of the Catholic clergy in the U. S. with town or diocese of residence).

List of Persons admitted to the Order of Deacons in the Protestant Episcopal Church in the United States of America from A.D. 1785 to A.D. 1857, Rt. Rev. George Burgess, D.D., 1874, at NYHS and NYPL; *Ibid.,* for 1858–1885, Rev. Elijah H. Downing, 1886, at NYPL (chronological and alphabetical, with ordination date and officiating bishop, also death date) (forms a complete list of Episcopal ministers, with clue to probable early residence through the bishop's name).

Archives of the General Convention: The Correspondence of John Henry Hobart, 1757–1811, ed. Arthur Lowndes, 6 vols., 1911–12 (includes editorial notes on laymen or clergymen mentioned; NYHS has unpublished remainder of Episcopal Bishop Hobart's correspondence to his death in 1830).

Bulletin of the General Theological Seminary (Episcopal), 1924 (alumni and nongraduates 1822–1924).

Alumni Catalogue of the Union Theological Seminary in the City of New York (Presbyterian), *1836–1926,* Rev. Charles R. Gillett, 1926.

Inventory of the Church Archives in New York City, W.P.A.: volumes on eight denominations (for description, see Church records section of this Guide); their alphabetical lists of first and current ministers identify many churches' ministers because so many churches were started throughout the 19th century.

DIRECTORIES

New kinds of directories of biographical interest are mainly social; for related items, see also Varied Memberships and Wealth in the Other Name Lists section of this Guide. Directories of foreign residents will be found under Origin in the Non-Native New Yorker section. Checklists and sample directories for areas outside the city are listed in the Removals from New York City section of this Guide's Supplement.

The McAllister 400, Melville Publishing Co., 1892, at NYHS (lists the 611 "now prominently to the front . . . either by gold, brains, or beauty").

Elite Private Address and Carriage Directory (title varies), pr. 1874–1892, Phillips, Andrade & Co. (arranged by streets and house numbers).

The List: A Visiting and Shopping Directory for the season of . . ., 1879–1884 variously at NYGB, NYPL, and NYHS.

Social Register: New York, issues from April 1887 at NYHS, from (annual) 1888 at NYPL, from Feb. 1898 at NYGB (includes lists of marriages and deaths for the year; in early issues, engagements also; college and club affiliations; winter and summer residences).

Western Union Telegraph Directory, 1874 at NYPL; *Tariff Book and General Directory,* American District Telegraph Company, 1891, at NYHS (has special lists with addresses, e.g. clubhouses, consulates, French flats and apartment houses, office buildings; includes Brooklyn, Jersey City, and Hoboken).

Official House Directory of N.Y.C. for the Year 1882 . . ., at NYPL: "aim . . . to show at a glance the names of the adult male residents in any house in New York" (arranged as was the city's list of registered voters — see Voting section of this Guide).

Chronological and alphabetical checklist of the city's directories 1653–1900 at NYPL, in NYPL *Bulletin* for 1901, 5:190–95.
Telephone books, at NYPL and NYHS (first New York City telephone directory was issued October 1878).

OCCUPATIONAL NAME LISTS AND BIOGRAPHICAL SKETCHES

Reference should also be made to Biographical Compendiums in the Secondary Sources section of this Guide's Supplement.

COMPENDIUMS

Volume commemorating the Creation of The Second City of the World: City of New York [Edward H. Hall], The Republic Press, 1898 (has many biographical paragraphs and photographs grouped under: charter and city commissions, city administration, lawyers, bench and bar, public accounting, physicians and surgeons).
Twitt's Directory of Prominent Business Men in New-York, 1858 (advertisements of and descriptive paragraph on each business establishment), at NYPL and NYHS.
History and Commerce of New York, American Publishing & Engraving Co., 2d ed., 1891 (paragraphs on business firms and their proprietors).
New York's Great Industries . . . its Leading Merchants and Manufacturers, ed. Richard Edwards, 2 vols., 1884–85.
"Metropolitan Industry: How the Advent of Peace affects Production and Prices": series in the *New York Times* of June and July 1865 (mentions various firms).
American Bibliography, Charles Evans — correction of previous listing: year 1820 for project's end abandoned; it will be completed through 1800 with publication c1953 of vol. 13.

FIREMEN

Volunteer fire company rolls (including fire wardens and engineers) 1784–1880, in 26 vols.
Mutual Hook & Ladder Co. No. 1: minutes, roll, fires, etc., 1799–1865, in 6 vols.
Firemen's affidavit register (certifying discharge of his duty as a volunteer), 1856–68, in 2 vols.
All the above, formerly in the City Clerk's office, are now in the Municipal Archives and Records Center.
History of the New York Fire Department, Lowell M. Limpus, 1940.

BANKERS

Merchants' and Bankers' Almanac, starting 1860, at NYHS (includes lists of banks and their officers by city and state, same for private bankers, lists of bankers in N.Y.C. with addresses, some biographical sketches; 1860 issue lists members of the N. Y. stock board; 1870 issue lists N, Y. C. bankers and brokers, indicating if member of the stock or gold exchange, etc.).

STOCK BROKERS

See Bankers above.

CREDIT REPORTERS

Centennial of the Birth of Impartial Credit Reporting — an American Idea: The Mercantile Agency established 1842, Dun & Bradstreet, Inc., 1941, at NYPL.

ACCOUNTANTS

See Compendiums above.
The American Association of Public Accountants: Its First Twenty Years, 1886–1906, MS c1953 by Norman E. Webster, N. Y. C. (may be printed later) (Who's Who sketches of 266 members, also of some practitioners in the 1860's and 1870's).

MERCHANTS

Lives of American Merchants, Freeman Hunt, N. Y. 1856.
Merchants Club of New York, c1871, at NYHS (membership list).
Maritime Association of the Port of New York, 1883, at NYHS (lists 1,999 members in 55 kinds of business, with their firm, kind of business and address).
Merchants of our Second Century; Representative Americans. Biographical Sketches ..., C. F. Deihm, vol. 1 (all issued), 1889, at NYPL (on N.Y.C. merchants, many born elsewhere).

INDUSTRIES AND MANUFACTURING

History of the New York Swamp, Frank W. Norcross, 1901 (families in N. Y. C.'s leather industry).
Hide and Leather Club of New York, 1880, at NYHS (membership list).
American Institute of the City of New York (org. 1828): publications and 99 cases of inventoried records, at NYHS (especially in early period, encouraged inventions and science through its annual exhibitions and medals).

ARTISTS AND DESIGNERS

See Architects and Building Trades below.

ARCHITECTS AND BUILDING TRADES

Obituaries of architects, artists, art patrons, and sculptors: card index at Avery Architectural Library, Columbia University (about 12,000 cards, alphabetical, of national scope, from 20th century newspapers and periodicals, also 19th century periodicals).
History of Architecture and the Building Trades of Greater New York, 2 vols., Union History Co., 1899, at NYPL (includes data on the early occupational associations and trade unions, institutes, and building supply firms).
Building Trades Club, 1892; *Hardware Club of New York*, 1894 (membership lists) at NYHS.
See also Carpenters, and Tradesmen and Mechanics in this section of the main Guide.

BOOKSELLERS, PRINTERS, AND PUBLISHERS

Type Founders, Copperplate Printers, Stereotypers, Writing and Printing Ink Manufacturers and Sellers in N. Y. C. 1759–1820, Harry B. Weiss, in NYPL *Bulletin* (1951–52), 53:471–83, 54:383–94.
New York Press Club: Constitution, By-Laws and List of Members, 1891, at NYHS (org. 1872; lists members with address or name of journal).
See also Compendiums above.

THE STAGE

The Players, 1892 (org. 1888; lists members living and deceased).

MUSICIANS

A Decade in the Musical History of New York (City), 1800 to 1810, Lois Mary Fellows, MS 1938 Master's thesis in Columbia University's History Dep't. library.

JUDGES

For chancellors, justices, and judges, see under The Courts in this Guide's Supplement.

PHYSICIANS

Many changes occurred in the licensing, etc., of physicians in the period 1872–1907, including an 1880 law requiring physicians to register their licenses with the county clerk and an 1890 law which limited to the Regents the power to grant licenses to practise medicine.

Physicians and surgeons affidavits (books of chronological affidavits signed by the doctor, giving proofs that he had been admitted to practise) 1874–1880 unindexed, 1880–1951 with index register, at N. Y. County Clerk's office.

College of Physicians and Surgeons, New York and its Founders, Officers, Instructors, Benefactors and Alumni: A History, ed. John Shrady, 2 vols. [no date], at NYGB.

Short Sketch of the New York Medical College, Edwin H. Davis, 1883 (lists officers and graduates during its existence in N. Y. C., 1850–1864).

History of the Long Island College Hospital and its Graduates, Joseph H. Raymond, M.D., 1899 (biographical sketches for classes of 1860–99 of this Brooklyn medical college).

OTHER NAME LISTS: EDUCATION, MEMBERSHIPS, WEALTH, ETC.

EDUCATION AND TEACHING

New York Society of Associated Teachers: Minutes 1794–1807, formerly at Secretary of State's office, now at NYSL, 1 vol.

Historical and Statistical Record of the University of the State of New York . . . 1784 to 1884, Franklin B. Hough, 1885 (lists honorary degrees conferred by the Regents, 4 of the 8 groups being M.D.s, the largest group based on nomination of the State Medical Society after 1840).

Columbiana collection at Low Memorial Library, Columbia University (extensive biographical data on officers and alumni).

General Alumni Catalogue of New York University, 1833–1906, 3 vol. ed. 1906–08 (more useful biographies than in the 1916 ed.).

Rutgers College, New Brunswick, N. J., General Catalogue includes graduates of the Rutgers Medical College, in New York City.

Hobart College, General Catalogue of Officers, Graduates and Students, 1825–1897, Geneva, N. Y., 1897 (upstate Episcopal college including a medical school 1834–1872).

History of the University Club, 1865–1915, James W. Alexander, 1915 (rolls of members in 1865 and 1879; alphabetical list of members 1879–1914 with dates of admission and death).

Harvard Club of N. Y. C.: List of the Members, 1877, at NYHS (org. 1865; lists 205 members with addresses).

LITERARY LIFE

New York Athenaeum: Minutes 1824–1840, at New York Society Library (53 E. 79th St.).

Authors' Club, New York, 1882–1932, at NYHS.

MASONIC LODGES

Winchester's annual Masonic Directory for the State of New-York, 1860, at NYPL (lists lodges by name and number, town and county, with names of the master and secretary of each).

VARIED MEMBERSHIPS

For societies indicative of origin, see Origin outside of New York City; for patriotic societies concerning the wars, see Military Records section of this Guide.

The Clubs of New York: with an account of the origin, . . . and membership of the leading clubs, Francis G. Fairchild, 1873, at NYPL (for 13 clubs).

American Jockey Club: List of Members and Rules, 1873.

Amateur Comedy Club, 1884, at NYHS (membership list).

Club Men of New York, The Republic Press, 1903, at NYGB (506-page alphabetical name list, with occupation, club, business and home addresses — often outside N. Y. C.).

Greek Letter Men of New York, Will J. Maxwell, 1899, at NYGB (each fraternity's members with addresses and photographs).

American Institute of the City of New York: *Catalogue of the Life and Annual Members 1868*, at NYHS (org. 1828).

N. Y. Horticultural Society, 1881 at NYHS (membership list).

American Seamen's Friend Society: 6th Annual Report 1833, at NYHS.
Female Missionary Society for the Poor of the City of New-York: Second Anni-
versary Report, 1818 at NYPL (lists of feminine subscribers).

WEALTH

For some records of those who lost their wealth, see Apprentices
and the Poor in this Guide's Supplement.

1844–1854 *Detailed Statement of Unpaid Personal Taxes for the Years 1844 to*
        1854 incl., N. Y. County Board of Supervisors, 1855, at NYPL (names by
        year, ward, and street).
1856–57 *Boyd's New York City Tax-Book; being a list of Persons, Corporations*
        & Co-Partnerships resident and non-resident who were taxed according to the
        Assessors' Books 1856 & '57 (1857), at NYPL (real estate and personal
        estate taxes).
The Rich Men of New York, Reuben Vose, 1861–62, at NYHS (alphabetical lists
        of individuals and firms, with kind of business and estimate of wealth).
1866 Dep't. of Internal Revenue's report: alphabetical list of N. Y. C. resi-
        dents, by districts and wards, whose incomes for the year ending May 1866
        exceeded $4,000, with the amount opposite each name, in *New-York Daily*
        Tribune of Aug. 11, 1866 (see mounted clippings for seven wards at NYGB).

SECONDARY AND OTHER SOURCES

The compilations other than encyclopedias previously mentioned
in the first paragraph of this section are mostly listed in full in this
Guide's Supplement, either in this section under Biographical Compendiums or in the Removals from New York City section (Spooner,
not Cutler, being the name of one compiler). However, the main
Guide describes Stokes and Bonner, the latter in the Name Lists
and Biographical Sketches by Occupation section.

GUIDES TO RECORDS AND DEPOSITORIES

Local Indexes in American Libraries: A Union List of Unpublished Indexes, ed.
        Norma Olin Ireland, Amer. Library Ass'n., 1947;
        Local indexes in New York libraries, mim.
Guide to the Reference Collections of The New York Public Library, Karl Brown,
        1941.
Dictionary of Books relating to America, Joseph Sabin: see esp. vol. 13 (1881),
        pp. 212–285 for N. Y. C. items, anonymous or official (otherwise listed under
        the author).
List of New York Almanacs 1694–1850, A. J. Wall, in NYPL *Bulletin* for 1920,
        v. 24.
Chronological List of Magazines 1741–1849, in *A History of American Maga-*
        zines, Frank L. Mott, 1930.

ACCOUNTS OF THE CITY, ITS LOCAL SECTIONS AND INSTITUTIONS

King's Handbook of New York City, Moses King, 1893 (over 1,000 illustrations;
        paragraphs on many hotels, churches, hospitals, business firms, charities,
        institutions, etc.).
New York, an American City, 1783–1803, Sidney I. Pomerantz, 1938 (good bib-
        liography).
The Charities of New York, Brooklyn, and Staten Island, Hy. J. Camman & Hugh
        N. Camp, 1868, at NYGB (each institution's founders, aims and current
        officials).
New York and its Institutions, 1609–1872, John F. Richmond, 1872 (includes
        municipal and private charitable institutions, mainly of mid-19th century).
Directory to the Charities of New York, 1873, at NYPL; *Classified and Descrip-*
        tive Directory to the Charitable and Beneficent Societies and Institutions of
        N. Y. C., 2d ed. 1887, at NYGB.
Civic Bibliography for Greater New York, James B. Reynolds, 1911.

American Diaries: An Annotated Bibliography of American Diaries prior to the Year 1861, Wm. Matthews, in University of California Publications in English, v. 16 (1945) (chronological, with author index; omits journals and MS diaries).

GUIDES TO PORTRAITS

Catalogue of the Works of Art belonging to the City of New York, Art Commission of the City of New York, 2 vols., 1909 and 1920 (3rd vol. in prep.).

BIOGRAPHICAL COMPENDIUMS

Famous Families of New York (City), Margherita A. Hamm, 2 vols., 1901.
Historic Homes and Institutions and Genealogical and Family History of New York (City), Wm. S. Pelletreau, 1907, vols. 3 and 4.
Historic Families of America, ed. Walter W. Spooner, 3 vols., 1907–08.
American Biographical Notes, being Short Notices of Deceased Persons, chiefly those not included in Allen's or in Drake's Biographical Dictionaries, Franklin B. Hough, 1875 (alphabetical, of national scope; some items from unusual sources, many are death notices from upstate New York newspapers).
Universities and Their Sons, ed. Joseph L. Chamberlain, 5 vols. 1898–1900 (biographies of alumni of Harvard, Yale, Princeton, and Columbia).
Genealogies of American Society, in *Town Topics,* issues for 1915–1919: typed index at NYPL (charts showing recent generations).
Who was Who in America, 1897–1942, and *1943–1950,* 2 vols.
Who's Who in New York City and State, 1st ed., 1904.
Encyclopaedia of Contemporary Biography of New York State, 1878–90, in 6 vols.
New York, The Metropolis, its Noted Business and Professional Men [John F. Sprague], 1893.[67]
Off-Hand Portraits of Prominent New Yorkers, Stephen Fiske, 1894.
America's Successful Men of Affairs, ed. Henry Hall, vol. 1 (all issued) 1895, N. Y. Tribune (on N. Y. C. men).
Makers of New York . . . Portraits and Sketches of the most eminent citizens of New York, ed. Charles Morris, 1895 (N. Y. C. men born in 18th and 19th centuries).[67]
Men of Affairs in New York (City) [Charles Morris], 1895.[67]
Prominent Families of New York (City) [ed. Lyman H. Weeks), revised ed., 1898.
The Men of New York (State), in 2 vols. 1898, Geo. E. Matthews & Co., Buffalo (Manhattan, 2:11–76).
Leslie's History of the Greater New York [Daniel Van Pelt, 1898–99], vols. 3 and 4.[67]
Biographical Directory of the State of New York, 1900 (1900) (12,000 brief paragraphs).
New York State's Prominent and Progressive Men, Mitchell C. Harrison, 2 vols., N. Y. Tribune, 1900.[67]
The Book of New York: 40 Years' Recollections of the American Metropolis, Julius Chambers, Editor of the N. Y. Herald and the N. Y. World, 1912 (biographical accounts).[67]
Herringshaw's City Blue Book of Biography: New Yorkers of 1917 — Ten Thousand Biographies, ed. Mae Felts Herringshaw, 1917.
See also Occupational Name Lists and Biographical Sketches section of this Guide.

THE NON-NATIVE NEW YORKER

In the search for origin, it is sometimes useful to look in the compendiums on families ancestrally New Yorkers. For this reason and because other ancestral societies are in this section, memberships of The Holland and the St. Nicholas societies are listed here

---

[67] Includes many photographs of individuals.

as well as those indicative of recent foreign and out-of-state origin. See the Military Records section for patriotic societies concerning the wars.

The Holland Society of New York: Year Books (include membership lists and obituaries) (org. 1875; limited to descent in the male line from a resident of the Dutch colony in North America prior to 1675).

Ohio Society of New York: Constitution and By-Laws, Officers and Members, 1888 and 1903 (lists of resident and non-resident members with address and former or present home in Ohio; the later issue has *In memoriam* list with death dates from org. 1886).

New York Southern Society: Fifth Annual Report (1891); *Year Book of . . . for 1911–12* (org. 1885, lists of resident and non-resident members with address, the later issue giving state of birth or descent).

The Pennsylvania Society of New York: First Annual Festival, 1899 (membership list).

Scots and Scots' Descendants in America, ed. Donald MacDougall, c1917 (good bibliography).

Scotland's Mark on America, George F. Black, 1921 (biographical notices grouped by occupation).

Irish-American Miscellany, relating largely to New York City and vicinity . . ., John D. Crimmins, 1905, at NYPL (many more than 500 biographical accounts, of other people than in his 1902 work already cited in this Guide).

Deutschen Gesellschaft der Stadt New York: Jahres-Bericht . . . für 1874 (1875), at NYHS (long list of members with their contributions and N. Y. C. home addresses).

Geschichte des Vereins Deutscher Liederkrans in New York, Hermann Mosenthal, 1897 (includes membership list with admission dates).

Geschichte des Deutschthums von New York, von 1848 . . ., Theodor Lemke, 1891, at NYPL (biographies and photographs).

Das deutsche Element der Stadt New York: Biographisches Jahrbuch der Deutsch-Amerikaner New Yorks, Otto Spengler, 1913, at NYHS (genealogical summaries).

Almanach et Directorium Français des Etats-Unis pour L'Année 1857, N. Y., at NYHS (classified business directory of professions and trades in N. Y. C. with advertisements; the same and a general directory of French people, grouped into 31 towns of the U. S. and Canada but especially in N. Y. C.).

Directory français et Guide des affaires . . . Residents français a New-York et aus environs . . ., Augustin P. Maugé, N. Y. 1864, at NYPL.

Guide du Français a New York, Brooklyn et les Environs, N. Y. Tribune, 1880, at NYPL (has alphabetical directory of French, Swiss, Belgian, Canadian, etc., residents forming the French language colony in N. Y. C., Brooklyn, and Paterson, N. J.).

Guida Manuale dell' Italiano a New York 1882–83, Fratelli Metelli, at NYPL (has section on the Italian colony, and alphabetical directory of Italians with occupation and address).

Four Centuries of Italian-American History, Giovanni E. Schiavo, 1952.

Norwegians in New York, 1825–1925, A. N. Rygg, c1941 (includes biographical accounts).

Emigrants from Scotland to America, 1774–1775: copied from a bundle of Treasury papers in the Public Record Office, London, MS by Viola Root Cameron 1930 at NYPL.

Shipping & Commercial List, newspaper printed 1815–1926 in N. Y. C., usually semi-weekly, at NYPL (useful for arrival dates of ships, etc., enabling a search of their passenger lists at the National Archives, Washington, D. C.).

For fact of naturalization, see also the Voting section in this Guide's Supplement.

STATE AND FEDERAL CENSUS RECORDS

The decennial census records of the Federal government for 1790 through 1840 merely name the head of the household and give figures for the number of that household's individuals in categories that vary with the census but that may be summarized as: age groups, sex, color, free or slave. Additional statistics in certain censuses are: 1820 and 1830, foreigners not naturalized; 1820, number of persons engaged in agriculture, commerce, or manufacture, and 1840, number of persons in each family engaged in . . . occupation to be filled in; 1830, white persons deaf and dumb or blind; and 1840 (printed, see Military Records section of this Guide), pensioners for Revolutionary or military services by name and age.

Starting with the 1850 census all members of a household are listed by name; starting with the 1880 census, the relationship of each to the head of the family is given. Other genealogical information in these later Federal censuses consist of: 1850 on, age, birthplace, and occupation; 1870, whether either parent is of foreign birth, and 1880, birthplace of each parent; 1850, 1860, 1880, whether married within the year, and 1880, whether single, married, divorced or widowed; 1880, street name and house number. In each instance, the relationship given is not limited to wife, daughter, etc., but includes servant, boarder, etc., and requested information on birthplace is merely the state or territory of the United States, or if of foreign birth, the country. These late nineteenth century censuses also give varying statistical data on color (or race), litaracy and schooling, economic status, and medical condition. Such items can be important, e.g., the "cannot write" column, if a "family record" is submitted in proof of relationship to a deceased person by an individual claiming right to inherit.

The 1850 Federal census of the city is now available on microfilm at both the NYGB and NYPL,[68] and the 1880 on microfilm at the D.A.R. library in Washington, D. C. The Federal census schedules through 1870 are available for public use at the National Archives, as previously stated; that for 1890 was burned; that for 1880 is in too poor physical condition to permit public use and inquiries thereon must be directed to the Bureau of the Census, Washington, 25, D. C.

Successful use of the voluminous 1880 Federal census of the city is facilitated by: (1) Bureau of the Census' private alphabetical index of those households in New York State having children less than ten years old; (2) National Archives and Records Service' locater (available on microfilm at NYGB), which describes the exact bounds of the census' 681 enumeration districts in Manhattan, and identifies each with an election district (having the same bounds except in about eight instances) and with a larger assembly district and ward of the city; (3) description and maps of the election districts as established July 22, 1879, at NYPL and NYHS (see Voting section of this Guide's Supplement); (4) list of registered voters in the city for 1880 by election districts and streets, at NYPL and NYHS (see *Ibid.*); (5) elite directory by streets and a regular city directory for 1880/1 (or possibly 1879/80); and (6) the check provided by the fact that this census gives the street name and house number of each household's dwelling, so that the wrong person with the same name need not be considered.

Similar facilities are not available for the earlier Federal censuses. Pending a project of mine for readier identification of census divisions with the city's streets and districts designed to minimize the frequent negative reports on census searches of the city schedules, I can give the following help. The 1870 census schedules are broken down by election districts, but not so for 1850 or 1860 although some of the latter census' divisions may correspond. See the Voting section of this Guide's Supplement for material that may be of aid in restricting the part of the census to be searched.

The Voting section might well be consulted also in connection with the state census of 1855, previously discussed.

---

[68] Both libraries have on microfilm the 1850 census for the present five boroughs of Greater N. Y. C.; for Long Island and Westchester County.

MAPS, STREET, AND LAND RECORDS

Minutes of the New Loan Office, 1792–c1823, original liber at the N. Y. County Clerk's office, Hall of Records (under the 1792 act for lending moneys of New York State, secured by mortgage on improved lands in the county then in the actual occupation of the borrower).[69]

Maps showing the following administrative districts (some changing annually): aldermanic, assembly, civil and police justices', congressional, councilmanic, election, school, senate, and ward, with the streets therein — printed since c1866 by N. Y. County Board of Supervisors, Board of Canvassers, Board of Police, and Board of Elections (see Voting section of this Guide's Supplement, which also gives an 1857 map).

"Changed House Numbers and Lost Street Names in New York of the early Nineteenth Century and later", Hy. B. Hoffman, in NYHS *Quarterly Bulletin* for 1937, 21:67–92.

See the section Printed Deed Indexes.

MILITARY RECORDS

Authoritative Civil War records of various kinds are innumerable. The important ones are presented here, together with records of the Spanish-American War and a few additions for the earlier period.

Card index of muster rolls in widely scattered printed sources, arranged by state and by war, covering the 17th through 19th centuries, compiled by Sylvester L. Vigilante and Daniel C. Haskell, at NYPL.

Some New York Veterans of the American Revolution, 1790–1855, John E. Bowman, 1928, MS at NYPL (alphabetical, mostly death notices from Boston and Vermont newspapers).

Pierce's Register on pp. 149–172 of *Seventeenth Report of the National D.A.R.*, 1915 (U. S. Senate Doc. 988, 63rd Congr., 3d Sess.) (alphabetical list of Continental Army officers and soldiers to whom certificates were issued 1783–85 by John Pierce, U. S. Paymaster General, to settle unpaid sums; the detailed records do not exist).

Disabled pensioners — List of persons returned by the District Judge of N. Y. as placed on the pension list or as not to be placed pending additional specified evidence; also those rejected for other states, under the 1792 act, in *N. Y. Daily Advertiser*, issue of July 24, 1794 (cf. differing lists in *American State Papers, Class IX Claims*).

Pensions under the 1828 act: master alphabetical list for the nation, giving *both* state of service and 1828 residence, pr. in *D.A.R. Magazine*, April 1953, pp. 561–74.

Pension application records, Old Wars Series, for disability or death in service in the wars and lesser engagements (such as the Barbary pirates) between the Revolution and the Civil War: at the National Archives, microfilm index just obtained by the NYPL.

Report of the Secretary of the Navy with statement showing the Operations of the Navy Pension Fund, 1828, 24 pp., Senate Doc. 139, 20th Congr., 1st Sess., at NYPL (alphabetical list of navy pensioners for each state, giving rank; also list of widow and orphan pensioners) (pensions, Old War Series, for disability or death in service since the Revolution).

Report of the Secretary of the Interior with a statement of rejected or suspended applications for pensions, 1852, Exec. Doc. 37, 32d Congr., 1st Sess., at NYPL (names alphabetical by states, with village and county of residence; many widows listed as married later than the military service).

Civil War federal pension records at the National Archives, Washington, D. C.: this war's basic pension acts are 1890 and 1907, the printed 1883 list of pensioners (*op. cit.*) including only service-disabled soldiers of this war.

---

[69] The minutes are in the form of chronologically entered mortgages having the original signatures. with the name crossed out when the mortgage was cancelled.

Register of Officers and Agents, civil, military and naval in the service of the United States together with . . . Ships belonging to the United States and when and where built, biennial 1816–1921, at NYPL.

The New-York State Register, Roger Sherman Skinner, 1830 (militia of the state with all officers down through Major, by regiment, brigade and division, pp. 341–65). Subsequent N. Y. State Registers by other editors list generals with their addresses.

New York State Adjutant General's Office; Annual Report of, for the years 1834 to date, at NYPL.
    1857–1919 include the Register, e.g. for 1857, pp. 78–247: Roster of the Military Force of the State of New York (officers' names grouped by unit and rank down through 2d lieutenants, with dates of commission, also town and county of residence).

Lists of killed and wounded in Mexico in the 1st Regiment of U. S. Volunteers of N. Y. commanded by Col. Ward Burnett, and of its casualties Dec. 3, 1846–Aug. 1, 1848, in *Annual Report of the New York State Adjutant General's Office for 1847* and *1848* (1848–49), at NYPL.

Registers of New York regiments in the War of Rebellion, in Supplementary volumes of *Annual Report of the New York State Adjutant General's Office for* 1893–1905, 43 vols.: (regiments of infantry #1–#194, of cavalry #1–#26, of artillery #1–#16, and other units) (arranged by units are military summaries for each man — officer, non-commissioned, and private — with his age).

Record of the commissioned officers, non-commissioned officers and privates of the regiments which were organized in the State of New York and called into the service of the United States to assist in suppressing the rebellion . . . 1861, as taken from the Muster-in Rolls on file in the Adjutant General's Office, State of New York, 1864–68, 8 vols. (those who volunteered to go forth to fight).

New York in the War of the Rebellion, 1861 to 1865, General Frederick Phisterer, 3d ed., 5 vols. + index vol., 1912 (the standard work for officers: section on officers who died in the service; military summary for each unit and for each of its officers arranged by units).

State Historian of the State of New York: Second and *Third Annual Report of,* for 1896 and 1897, Albany 1897–98 (engagements of various New York military units in the Civil War, 2:29–131, 3:13–128; burials of the 141st N. Y. Volunteers in the national cemetery at Marietta, Ga., 2:957–61).

Final Report on the Battlefield of Gettysburg, 1900, 3 vols.

Dedication of the New York State Monument on the Battlefield of Antietam, 1923.

Report on the New York Monuments at Chattanooga, 1928
    the above three titles by the N. Y. State Monuments Commission for the battlefields of . . . (accounts of N. Y. units with their officers at these three battles, with those killed at Antietam, Md., and Chattanooga).

Pilgrimage to the Shrines of Patriotism . . ., Andersonville Monument Dedication Commission, N. Y., 1916 (alphabetical list of N. Y. State soldiers buried in Andersonville National Cemetery, Ga., with his unit, date and cause of death).[70]

The Arlington Dead: List of New-York Soldiers buried in the National Cemetery (1,568 N. Y. State soldiers listed alphabetically with regiment of each, in mounted newspaper clippings at NYGB from unidentified newspaper, headed per our correspondent, Washington, D. C., June 3, 1871) (Arlington Cemetery records its burials alphabetically and not by state; it knows of no printed list of its burials).

Regimental histories: histories have been printed for a great many New York regiments in the Civil War, some documented and some chatty.

Navy: List of Men enlisted in the U. S. Navy, April 15, 1861 to Feb. 24, 1864, at N. Y. C., transcribed from Official Records of the Receiving Ship "North Carolina" stationed at the Brooklyn Navy Yard by the N. Y. Volunteer Committee for the Provost Marshal's Dep't., MS at NYHS (alphabetical list of 26,418 men, with age, occupation, residence, and ship to which transferred).

---

[70] Andersonville was the largest of five Confederate prisons where the dead were buried.

Reports of the Special Committee on Volunteering and of the Committee on Substitutes and Relief, pr. in *Proceedings of the New York County Board of Supervisors*, 1863 (Doc. #11, 91 pp.), and in *Documents of Ibid.*, 1864 (Doc. #6, 340 pp.; Doc. #38, 427 pp.; Doc. #11, 962 pp.), and 1866 (Doc. #12 in 2 vols.), at NYHS and NYPL: long name lists (one is of 32,787 men raised in the county) of volunteers for the army and navy, of army and navy recruits and reenlisted men who received or were not paid the county bounty; regiments or parts of regiments to which belong the reenlisted men paid or not paid the county bounty and their muster rolls in the Committee's possession (includes some Pa., La., and Ohio Volunteer reg'ts.); men reenlisted in the field and credited to New York County, classified by arm of service, regiment, etc.; names of drafted citizens relieved (grouped as policemen, firemen, militiamen, indigent persons), those who furnished substitutes, those for whom commutation was paid, and those actually mustered into the service; complete list of substitutes for army and navy, term enlisted, and name of person for whom the substitute was furnished with his ward and congressional district.

Records forming the basis of these printed documents.[71]

List of Delinquents of the Reserve Militia in the [1st through 99th Infantry, 1st and 3rd Cavalry, and 1st Artillery] Regimental District . . . who did not attend the Parade in the several Company Districts . . . September 1866, armed and equipped for inspection as the law directs, pr. in *Documents of the New York County Board of Supervisors*, 1866, vol. 3, Doc. #15, 898 pp.

U. S. Provost Marshal General's Office, N.Y.C.: *Names of Persons enrolled as liable to Military Duty under Act of Congress approved March 3, 1863* (short variant title — *Enrollment List*, printed separately for wards or congressional districts, mostly undated but are 1863), most at NYPL, some at NYHS: alphabetical lists of names with addresses for the 4th through 9th C.D.s, comprising the entire city[72] except for the 1st, 2nd, 4th, 6th, and 8th wards all in the 4th C.D. which are not known to exist.[72] (Exemptions from these lists were for: alienage, non-residence, non-suitable age, and permanent physical disability.)

Circulars listing persons in N. Y. C. liable to draft for the U. S. Army, issued by the N. Y. County Committee on Volunteering of the Supervisors Board, pr. in *N. Y. Daily Transcript* as Extras #1–#100, Dec. 10, 1864–Jan. 23, 1865, bound as one vol. at NYHS and NYPL: arranged by congressional districts and wards, alphabetical lists of names with residence, age, color, occupation, marital status, and state or country of birth. (Causes of exemption: over 45, under 20, alien who has not filed citizenship intention, substitute furnished, commutation paid, permanently physically disqualified or disabled, served 2 years in army or navy in present war and hon. discharged.)

Enrollments of Persons liable to Draft, 1862, 1863, 1864: bound numbers of *N. Y. Daily Transcript*.[71]

Names of prisoners, killed and wounded — newspaper clippings 1861–62.[71]

Civil War — various kinds of municipal records.[71]

Civil War — diaries, anecdotes, letters, enlistment books, logbooks, etc., at NYHS and NYPL.

Civil War — miscellaneous records of the Adjutant General's Office, Albany, including twelve bounty books (alphabetical).[73] Many of this office's records are now at NYSL, unindexed.[73]

Chronological list of the Laws of New York relating to the War of the Rebellion and Veterans of that War, 1861–1910, James D. Bell & W. B. Cook, Jr., 1910, at NYPL.

---

[71] Stokes, VI: 196, and see note 25 of this Guide.

[72] See map of the wards and C.D.s in *Documents of the New York County Board of Supervisors*, 1866, v. 3, Doc. #14, map p. 58, and also Sabin, *op. cit.*, 13:259. Sabin incorrectly grouped in N.Y.C. the 3rd C.D. of Brooklyn.

[73] For description, see H. L. Osgood. *op. cit.*, pp. 125–27; also W.P.A. *Guide to . . . MS Collections in New York State*, p. 30.

Political History of New York State during the period of the Civil War, Sidney D. Brummer, 1911.

Communication of the Comptroller . . . on account of the Damage by Riots of 1863, pr. in *Documents of the New York County Board of Supervisors*, 1868, Doc. #13, 1082 pp. (sworn statements of particulars of each claim include some biographical items).

Introduction to the Papers of the New York Prize Court, 1861–1865, Madeline R. Robinton, 1945.

War of the Rebellion: . . . Official Records of the Union and Confederate Armies, pub. under the Secretary of War, 1880–1901, in 130 vols. incl. index vol.

Official Record of the Union and Confederate Navies in the War of the Rebellion, U. S. Navy Dep't., 1894–1922, in 30 vols. + index vol., 1927.

New York in the Spanish American War: part of the Report of the Adjutant-General of the State for 1900, in 3 vols., 1900 (military summary for each regiment and for each of its soldiers, including age); *Index to* . . ., Chauncey W. Herrick, 1914.

New York and the War with Spain: History of the Empire State Regiments — Annual Report of the State Historian, 1903.

History of the First Battalion, Naval Militia New York, 1891–1911, Telfair M. Minton, 1911 (its war roster of the 1898 war includes seamen and landsmen and ships on which each served; roll of honor 1891–1911, with rank and dates of entry and discharge, includes seamen).

The U.S.S. Yankee on the Cuban Blockade 1898, N. Y. 1928 (full biographical accounts of officers and crew of this ship recruited from N. Y. C., pp. 104–69).

Regimental histories of the part taken in the Spanish-American War.

Military Album containing over 1,000 Portraits of Commissioned Officers who served in the Spanish-American War, 1902, at NYPL (navy and army, volunteers and regulars).

Alphabetical List of Battles, 1754–1900, compiled from official records, Newton A. Strait, 2d ed., 1914 (battles engaged in by the U. S. or part of it; also chronological summary of related events).

U. S. Military Philosophical Society: Original minutes and records, membership lists, and papers written for the Society, including material on N. Y. C. defenses during the War of 1812, at NYHS: 4 vols., 1789–1813.

Seventh Regiment military library: given 1948 to NYHS with its own card catalog.

Aztec Club of 1847 (Military Society of the Mexican War): Constitution and list of members 1928, at NYPL (lists of members with military rank and corps, brevets for service in Mexico, civilian occupation, dates of election and death or residence if living, 1847–1928; similar data on officers killed in Mexico or who served in Mexico but were not members).

Military Order of the Loyal Legion of the U. S.: Roster of the Commandery of the State of New York . . . 1866–1917, at NYHS (for officers in the Civil War and descendants) (alphabetical lists of names with rank, election date, address or death date, and — if transferred — the state to which or from which membership transferred).

Lineage books, rosters, publications, etc., of the D.A.R., S.A.R., S.R., G.A.R., etc.

Naval History Society collections: given to NYHS in 1925.

SPECIAL RECORDS AND ARCHIVES

In the past year the Municipal Archives and Records Center, under James Katsaros,[74] has received some records from the City Clerk's office, but none as yet that were separately itemized in the main part of this Guide. The status of City Clerk's and Comptroller's Office records, discussed in notes 20 and 25, remains correct.

---

[74] Correct spelling.

THE COURTS

The court system was extensively changed in 1895, and the new arrangement is not covered in this Guide.

History of the Court of Common Pleas of the City and County of New York, James W. Brooks, 1896, at NYPL (biographies of its judges, pp. 61–131).

The Council of Revision of the State of New York; its History, a History of the Courts with which its members were connected; Biographical Sketches of its Members; and its Vetoes, Alfred B. Street, 1859, at NYHS (eight courts; biographies of three chancellors, eight chief justices, and fifteen justices of the Supreme Court).

CITY CIVIL APPOINTMENTS AND ADMINISTRATION

Do not overlook the material in the annual *Valentine's Manuals*. Reference should also be made to the Compendiums and Firemen subsections of the Occupational Name Lists and Biographical Sketches section, and to Biographical Compendiums in the Secondary Sources section of this Guide. For administrative districts, refer to the Voting section and the Maps, Street and Land records section.

Civic Bibliography for Greater New York, James B. Reynolds, 1911.

Our Police Protectors: History of the New York Police from the earliest Period to the Present time, A. E. Costello, 2d ed., 1885 (biographical accounts and photographs; alphabetical list of Police Force members in the late 1800's with date appointed).

1840   *Names and places of abode of the mayor and members of the Common Council, and of officers holding appointments under them 1840*, N. Y. Common Council, 1840, at NYPL.

1843   *City Election Handbook: containing the returns of votes in each of the election districts and wards in the City of New York at the election November 1843; votes for Mayor from 1834 to 1843; list of office holders under the corporation and their salaries; naturalization law. . . .*, 1844.

1862–1870   *Complete Statement of the Official Canvass in detail giving the vote of every election district at the election of . . .*, New York County Board of Canvassers (give the votes for various candidates; some years include maps of the districts).

1873   *Cummins' Campaign guide and voters' directory of the City of New York*, J. Cummins, 1873 (list of principal officials in New York, whether city, county, state, or federal; sketches of leading parties, including lists of members of the General or Central Committee — by districts — of Tammany, Apollo Hall, and Republican parties in N. Y. C.).

1897   *Voters' directory: Concise and accurate information about all candidates for office in Greater New York at the approaching election*, N. Y. Evening Post, Oct. 1897.

1898   *The Brown Book: A Biographical Record of Public Officials of the City of New York for 1898–9*, pub. Martin B. Brown Co., 1899.

New York Daily News, 1855 on (strong Tammany newspaper; printed official and legal items and notices in 1850's).

New York Daily Transcript, 1859–1872, at NYHS (the city's official organ May 8, 1860 to June 4, 1872).

The City Record, June 24, 1873 on, at NYPL (the city's official journal; various Supplements issued separately, e.g., City and County Civil List starting 1900).

STATE CIVIL APPOINTMENTS AND LAWS

The New-York Annual Register, Edwin Williams, 1830 on, at NYHS (political and statistical data for the state including: list of steamboats, lines and routes; incorporated manufacturing companies and data on manufactories by county; colleges, academies, female seminaries, medical institutions, literary societies, etc.; also the state's civil and judicial list, military establishment and clergy (by town and denomination); attorneys' agents at Albany, N. Y. C., Utica and Canandaigua; list of practising attorneys by town; civil list of city governments; the federal civil, judicial, army, and navy lists.

The New-York State Register, annual continuation of the above under various editors.

Biographical Sketches of the State Officers and Members of the Legislature of the State of New York in 1858, Wm. D. Murphy (first of annual series continued with variant title by McElroy & McBride through 1876).

FEDERAL RECORDS

Federal office-holders in New York City are found listed in the city directories, the state registers, and various publications referred to in the preceding city and state sections of this Guide. *Official Registers of the United States* are indexed by name only after 1877.

Register of Officers and Agents, civil, military, and naval in the service of the United States together with . . . Ships belonging to the United States and when and where built, 1816 on, usually biennial (later called *Official Register of the U. S.*), at NYPL (include people stationed in New York such as custom house collectors, tax collectors, deputy postmasters and clerks, mail contractors; columns for each individual include state or country where born, town where employed, and compensation).
Outstanding collection of government publications at NYPL.

APPRENTICES AND THE POOR

Records of those who lost their wealth are included here.

Indices to Certificates of sheriff's sales filed in the office of the Clerk of the City and County of New York, 1820–1855, N. Y. County Records Commissioner, 1857, at NYPL.

Indices of insolvent assignments filed in the office of the Clerk of the City and County of New York through 1855, N. Y. County Records Commissioner, 1857 at NYPL.

Sheriffs' and U. S. Marshals' Certificates of Sale of Property in the City and County of New York filed in the office of the Clerk of the City and County of New York, 1820–1894, John S. Ames, former Official Searcher, 1894 at NYHS.
Register of discharges of insolvent debtors from prison by the Recorder of N. Y. C., 1811–13, 1816–18, in 2 packages at NYHS.

NEWSPAPERS

Indexes permit coverage of the many-page issues of the later period. For specialized newspapers in various fields, see the printed checklists previously listed in this Guide; only one is singled out below because its data is especially helpful.

New York Times — subject index 1851–1859 on microfilm at NYHS, and printed 1860, 1863–1905, 1913 on.
New York Daily Tribune — printed subject index 1875–1906.
New York Morning Herald — after the New York Post, it is the second best paper in which to find marriage and death notices; no index available to the public (a MS subject index 1873–1924 owned by the N. Y. Telegram was superficially extended back to c1840, including scanty, chronological list of obituaries from 1848 and of marriages from 1858).
Shipping & Commercial List, total run 1815–1926 under variant titles, printed in N. Y. C., usually semiweekly, at NYPL (gives ship arrivals at and destinations for various ports; ship disasters; captain and agent, consignee or owner of each ship; commodity prices and duties, imports by ship and merchant, exports, public commodity sales, and market review).

Most late nineteenth century publications containing biographical notices include photographs of individuals; see especially those listed under Biographical Compendiums in the Secondary Sources section of this Guide's Supplement. Books composed solely of such photographs are:

Notable New Yorkers of 1896–1899, Moses King, 1899 (N. Y. C. men).

Military Album containing over 1,000 Portraits of Commissioned officers who served in the Spanish-American War, 1902.

VOTING

This section includes material concerning voters and voting from various angles. It will have many uses, for example, election district[75] maps and registries of voters are helpful preliminaries to census searching, membership in Tammany or other democratic organizations suggests the possibility of city office-holders, and the house by house listing in the registries of voters gives a man's neighbors and a clue to his economic standing. Attention is called to the Naturalization section of the main Guide.

Wards of N. Y. C.: history of, arranged chronologically, James Katsaros, 1950, MS in Municipal Reference Library branch of the NYPL.

1801   Electoral census, at NYSL.[76]

1808   Names of Persons who voted in the 3rd Ward, April 1808, with notations whether Federal, Democrat, or doubtful, at NYHS.[77]

1814, 1821   Electoral censuses, at NYSL and at the Comptroller's Office, N.Y.C.[76] The 1820 and 1830 Federal censuses list the number of foreigners in a household who are not naturalized.

1825   List of jurors in N. Y. C., at NYHS.[77]

1840–41   *Register of Electors of the 17th Ward*, 1840, and *Ibid.* of the 15th Ward, 1841, both at NYHS; *Ibid.* of the 10th Ward for 1840, N. Y. C. Registry Committee, 1841 at NYPL (names alphabetical with address and occupation and date each registered).

1842 on   Ordinances to divide N. Y. C. into election districts, etc., under an 1842 act of the legislature, in *Proceedings of the Boards of Aldermen and Councilmen* (or *Assistant Aldermen*) approved by the Mayor.

[1855]   *Ibid.* for 1853–54 (21:400–12) gives the bounds of the election districts in effect at the time of the June/July 1855 state census except for the 22nd Ward, which was redistricted during 1854 (22:15–21 and 264).

1855   State census, at N. Y. County Clerk's Office, says whether each adult is a native, naturalized voter, or alien, and gives the number of years resident in the city.[76]

1857   Map of senatorial and assembly election districts, now in Municipal Archives and Records Center (17 districts, showing ward division).

1859   *Amended Ordinance: Re-districting the city into election districts, with the E.D.s embraced within the 17 aldermanic districts,* Board of Councilmen (or Assistants) Oct. 1, 1859, Doc. #10 (1859), at NYPL (bounds but no maps).

1863–1865   Enrollment lists of those liable for the draft concern citizens only.[78]

1866–1870   Maps of wards and district divisions of the County of New York showing election districts as arranged Aug. 1, 1869, printed in *Documents of the New York County Board of Supervisors*, 1869, Doc. #9. Similarly for the other years.

---

[75] Election districts, determined annually, are often changed.

[76] See Census Records section of the main Guide.

[77] See Wealth and Miscellaneous Lists in the main Guide.

[78] See Military Records section.

1872   Earliest of annual maps of election districts at the Board of Elections; its enrollment lists do not start until 1902.
1872–1878   Registration of naturalized voters, formerly at Board of Elections, now in Municipal Archives and Records Center (alphabetical lists, by districts).
1874   *Registry of Voters in the City of New York, by wards, assembly and election districts*, John I. Davenport, at NYHS and NYPL.
1876   *Ibid., Vol. VII — 7th Assembly District 1876, portions of the 9th, 15th and 16th wards*, John I. Davenport, 1876, at NYHS.
1877   *Directory of the registered voters of the City of New York, arranged by streets and house numbers*, John I. Davenport, 1877, at NYHS and NYPL.
1879   *Election Districts of the several assembly districts of the City and County of New York and the boundaries thereof as established by the Board of Police, July 22, 1879* (1879), at NYHS and NYPL (includes maps).
1880   *List of Registered Voters in the City of New York for the Year 1880*, Committee of One Hundred on Democratic Re-organization, 1881, in 2 vols., at NYHS and NYPL (arranged by assembly and election districts, streets and house numbers).
1881–1903   *List of Registered Voters*, Supplement of the City Record, printed annually end of October or early November, at NYPL (arranged by assembly and election districts and address therein).
1884   *Republican enrollment for 1884: 11th Assembly district*, N. Y Evening Post printing office, 1884, at NYHS and NYPL.
1899 to date   *Transcript of the Enrollment Books* (later called *List of enrolled voters*), N. Y. C. Board of Elections, annual Supplement of the City Record, at NYPL (list of annually enrolled voters arranged alphabetically within each election district, and giving political affiliation).
Tammaniana, Society of Tammany, or Columbian Order in the City of New York, MS by Edwin P. Kilroe, at NYHS (members 1789–1924, alphabetical and chronological).
History of the Tammany Society, E. Vale Blake, 1901 (biographies of N. Y. Democrats and Tammany members of the late 19th century).
The Democratic Club of the City of New York, 1894, at NYHS (incorp. 1890; lists resident and non-resident members with addresses, also deceased members).
The Republican Club of the City of New York, 1889, at NYHS (org. 1879; lists 505 resident and non-resident members with addresses and date of joining).
Union League Club, Historical and Biographical, 1863–1900, Joseph Howard, Jr., 1900 (biographies and portraits of members, in early period invariably Republican).
Union League Club: In Memoriam Members March 9, 1933, N. Y. 1933, at NYPL (alphabetical list of deceased members from org. 1863, with dates of admission and death).
The Triumph of Reform: History of the Great Political Revolution Nov. 6, 1894, W. Ten Eyck Hardenbrook, at NYPL (various political groups, committees and clubs active for good government, with officials' photographs and biographical accounts).

REMOVALS FROM NEW YORK CITY

There is no short cut to tracing people who left New York City. Each case must be treated as a special problem. This section, necessarily fragmentary, is presented to stimulate the searcher into approaching his problem from different aspects.

The following nineteenth century records may give the person's new address:

Next of kin lists in the probate records

Land records, if property was sold after the removal

City directories, if removal was to the suburbs or if the business remained in town

Military and naval pension applications, whether granted or not
Cemetery records, of ownership interests in or for care of the plot
Membership records of the church, if dismissions or transfers were
noted
Files and alumni catalogs of the college or university
Membership records of patriotic societies, etc.
Bank records (if available) for the bank account, loan, or mortgage

Many people left New York for the suburbs or for northern and
western New York State. The lack of centralization of records[79]
makes this state a difficult one in which to do research without go-
ing to the county. If the county or area of removal is not known
and if the searcher is lucky, the desired name may turn up in
items such as the following, which might be used as "catch-all"
indexes in order to localize the missing individual or his family.

Biographical and portrait index to the state, county, and city histories of New
York State, Gunther E. Pohl, N. Y. C. (upon completion, to be in book form).
Lewis Historical Publishing Co. series: *Genealogical and Family History of Northern
New York*, 1910; *Ibid., for Central New York*, 1912; *Ibid., for Western New
York*, 1912 — each in 3 vols. and all by Wm. R. Cutter; *Ibid., of Southern
New York and Hudson River Valley*, Cuyler Reynolds, 3 vols., 1914; *Genealo-
gies of the State of New York — Long Island Edition*, Tunis G. Bergen, 3
vols., 1915; *Hudson-Mohawk Genealogical and Family Memoirs*, 4 vols., 1911.
American Families of Historic Lineage — Long Island Edition, ed. Wm. S. Pelle-
treau and John Howard Brown, 2 vols.
History of Long Island, Benjamin Thompson, 1st ed., 1839; 3rd ed., 1918.
Early Settlers of (Western) New York State, Their Ancestors and Descendants
(title varies), Janet Wethy Foley, 8 vols., 1934–42 (mostly records).
Ms Index of Personal Names contained in the *Historical and Statistical Gazetteer
of New York State* by J. H. French in 1860, compiled by Louis D. Scisco,
1937, at NYGB (the Gazeteer lists the first settlers of many towns).
*Complete Name Index to Pioneer History of the Holland Purchase of Western New
York by O. Turner 1849 and 1850*, compiled by LaVerne C. Cooley, 1946;
*Complete Name Index to History of the Pioneer Settlement of Phelps and
Gorham Purchase by O. Turner 1851*, compiled by LaVerne C. Cooley, 1946.
(These two purchases and the Military Tract comprised most of western
New York State).
*The Balloting Book, and other Documents relating to Military Bounty Lands, in
the State of New York*, 1825.
*Index of Awards on Claims of the Soldiers of the War of 1812, as audited and allowed
by the Adjutant and Inspector Generals* (of N. Y. under) . . . *Laws of 1859*,
Albany, 1860 (claims for federal pay for war service; certificates with affidavits for survivors in N. Y.'s Northern Collection District are now at
NYSL) (gives residence by town, county, and state; proves migration of
many to western N. Y. and over the U. S.) at NYHS and at NYSL.
*Calendar of New York Colonial Manuscripts, indorsed Land Papers, in the office
of the Secretary of State, 1643–1803*, Albany, 1864 (indexed digest of 63
volumes of manuscripts now at NYSL) (pp. 669–1025 for the period 1785–
1803 give claims by soldiers, petitions, affidavits, land locations, surveys,
etc., *re* vacant lands).
Card indexes of patents and deeds, by name and by location — county and
town, in the Land Office of the Department of State now at 164 State St.
Albany, N. Y.
*Digest of Claims and the Action thereon by the Legislature and the Canal Board,
together with the Awards made by the Board of Canal Appraisers, from 1818
to 1858*, S. P. Allen, Clerk of the Senate, 1858.

[79] Other than vital statistics, which since 1880 have been registered at the State Dep't. of Health,
Albany, for the state exclusive of Albany, Buffalo, New York, and Yonkers.

General Index to the Laws of the State of New York (especially for private claims).

Card index of marriage and death notices in upstate New York newspapers of about the period 1784–1834, compiled by Joseph Gavit and on loan at NYSL.

See also Biographical Compendiums in the Secondary Sources section, especially Hough for death notices from upstate New York newspapers.

D.A.R.: Graves of Revolutionary War Soldiers (and wives) buried in N. Y. State, MS volumes at NYSL.

Spencer's Roster of native sons, Alfred Spencer, c1941 ("For each locality of upstate New York a roster of its eminent sons and daughters, from earliest settlement to the present time", with dates and places of birth and death).

Index to the Public Records of the County of Albany, State of New York, 1630–1894, ed. Wheeler B. Melius & Frank H. Burnap: grantees, grantors, lis pendens, maps, mortgagors, 37 vols., printed, 1902–17.

Department of History and Archives, Montgomery County Archivist, Old Court House, Fonda, N. Y. (unusually good collection for central New York — old Montgomery Co.).[80]

Federal census records for entire New York State 1800, 1810 and 1830 on microfilm at NYSL; for entire state 1850 on microfilm at NYGB (just acquired). For 1850 census, see note 68 of this Guide.

State census records filed at the respective county clerk's office; some also at NYSL. See *An Inventory of New York State and Federal Census Records,* Edna Jacobsen, NYSL pub. Feb. 1942 (lists each county clerk's records).

Civil List . . . of the State of New York, indexed editions.

New York Mercantile Union Business Directory, 1850–51, S. French, at NYPL (classified business directory for the state, e.g. 2½ pp. of agents with exact address, grouped by counties and kinds of agent).

Westchester County Directory for 1860–61, Thomas Hutchinson, 1st ed., at NYPL (general directory of 5 towns, classified business directory of the county, and list of farmers by towns).

Northern New York Business Directory, 1867–68, Waite Bros. & Co., at NYPL (alphabetical for each town).

Boyd's Business directory of over one hundred villages in New York State, 1869 at NYPL.

New York Central and Hudson River Railway Classified Business Directory between New York and Albany for . . . 1884–85, at NYGB (arranged by towns).

Bender's Lawyers diary & directory for the State of New York, 1897–98, at NYPL.

See also mid-19th century gazetteers, and checklists of directories below.

For nearby regions outside the state, in New Jersey and Connecticut, I will only mention:

1850 Federal census of New Jersey, on microfilm at NYGB.

New Jersey Historical Society, Newark, N. J., has a card index of marriage and death notices in Newark newspapers.

Connecticut State Library, Hartford, Conn., has master card indexes for the state of vital records, church records (in process), gravestone inscriptions, marriage and death notices in newspapers, census records 1790–1850 (in process), and estates.

Westward migration is likewise difficult if the person's next state of residence is not known; New York had no western tracts like the Connecticut Reserve, and New Yorkers seem to have merely spread westward, the Gold Rush being an exception. One should not overlook the possibility of tracing the individual through his occupation, interests, or affiliations. The following may prove useful if only to suggest similar search in the area of the person's probable removal.

---

[80] W.P.A., *Guide to . . . MSS Collections in New York State,* pp. 109–14.

Minnesota Historical Society, St. Paul, Minn., has a very full alphabetical biographical file of current and especially of early Minnesotans and where they came from.

Michigan Pioneer and Historical Society's *Historical Collections.*

Detroit Society for Genealogical Research, Detroit, Michigan, issues a Magazine containing many names from the N. Y. C. area, and the Burton Historical Collection contains much unorganized material on the origin of Michigan people.

Wisconsin State Historical Society, Madison, has useful files.

"Wisconsin, New York's Daughter State", Edward P. Alexander, in *Wisconsin Magazine of History.*

Oregon State Library, Salem, Oregon, has a catalog listing many previous residents of Oregon. A New York State Society in Oregon formerly existed.

D.A.R.: specialized assembling of local material by local chapters of the D.A.R. is deposited in a designated library for that state, e.g., The Newberry Library in Chicago, Ill. The Sutro Branch of the California State Library, San Francisco, has "Pioneer Papers", in 12 vols. to date, compiled by the California D.A.R.

California pioneers' geographic origin: considerable unorganized material thereon is in both the Bancroft Library, University of California, Berkeley, and the Society of California Pioneers, San Francisco. The latter's *Centennial Roster . . . 1948* (org. 1850 for those who arrived before 1850 and their descendants) lists all members with date of arrival or name of arriving ancestor.

"Pioneer Register" in *History of California,* Hubert H. Bancroft.

The Argonauts of California by a Pioneer [C. W. Haskins], 1890: Appendix pp. 360–501 has thousands of names of pioneers (indexed by the Society of California Pioneers) in small alphabetical groups by membership (e.g. N. Y. C. Pioneer Ass'n.), emigrating company, or passenger list. The latter seem to be incomplete reprints from the newspapers, cf. *N. Y. Daily Tribune* of April 7, 1849 and *N. Y. Herald* of April 1, 1849.

D.A.R.: *Roster of Soldiers and Patriots of the American Revolution buried in Indiana,* 1938.

D.A.R.: *The Official Roster of the Soldiers of the American Revolution buried (or who lived) in the State of Ohio* [1929, 1938].

"Directories in the Library of Congress," Philip Mack Smith, in *The American Genealogist,* 13:46–53, 27:142 (gives the earliest date at LC for each town or other area).

"Early American Directories in the Library of . . . (NYHS)," in NYHS *Quarterly,* 30:92–104.

Town, county, and state directories at NYPL, arranged alphabetically in shelf lists for periods before and after 1870.

The Mercantile Agency: U. S. Business Directory for 1867, . . . merchants, manufacturers and traders . . ., R. G. Dun & Co., 822 pp. at NYPL (classified within sections for big cities and for states).

List of bank cashiers (treasurers) in the U. S., in *The Merchants' and Bankers' Almanac for 1861.*

Biographical dictionaries of accountants, of artists, of physicians, of ministers, etc.

Lineage Books of the D.A.R.

Military Order of the Loyal Legion: printed rosters showing members' transfers between its different state societies.

Federal census records, from 1850 on.

Other items already listed in this section or elsewhere in this Guide.

It may be noted that many who participated in the Gold Rush returned east and that some New Yorkers who went to Louisiana ended their days in New York. Many people came to New York City on business; upon retirement or a generation or so later, the family may have returned to the ancestral home area. Hence in the absence of a clue, one might look for membership in a regional organization, such as the New York Southern Society, with the idea of investigating a possible homeward trek.

Notes of a Voyage to California via Cape Horn . . . 1849–50, Samuel C. Upham, 1878 (has roll of members of The Associated Pioneers of the Territorial Days of California, org. 1875, for present residents of the Atlantic states, hdq. N. Y. C., with exact addresses of each in 1878).

See regional organizations listed in the section Origin outside of New York City.

ADDENDA AND CORRIGENDA

The previously itemized Court of Chancery records 1700–1847, Court of Probates Letters of administration 1778–1797, and various series of wills all filed with the Clerk of the Court of Appeals, Albany, have just been obtained on microfilm by NYGB.

1799 List of deaths in the city from the malignant fever July to Oct. 23, as reported to the Committee of Health, with occupations added, in *The Spectator*, N. Y., issues of Oct. 5 and Oct. 23, 1799.

1803 List of 610 deaths in the city from the malignant fever, July 29 to Oct. 29, in *The Spectator*, N. Y., issue of Nov. 9, 1803, and in *The Weekly Visitor*, issue of Nov. 5, 1803.

Intestate records before 1830 usually merely Letters of Administration libers giving deceased's occupation and sometimes relationship of administrator.

1830 Federal census of New York County on microfilm at NYHS, just acquired.

Revolutionary Soldiers resident or dying in Onondaga County, N. Y., Onondaga Historical Ass'n., 1913–14 (a county in the Military Tract surveyed for soldiers).

A List of the names of persons to whom military patents have issued out of the (N. Y. State) *Secretary's office and to whom delivered*, 1793, 25 pp., at NYPL (includes acreage; cf. slightly differing names in *The Balloting Book*).

Revolutionary War MSS now at NYSL: half of Comptroller's Office's 52 vols. salvaged from fire (see *New York in the Revolution, Supplement*, E. C. Knight, 1901, p. 273) (mostly vouchers or assignments of pay due, signed in late 1780's; post-war residence often shown but only name and rank printed).

Audited Accounts, 1783–1794, 2 vols. (for payments of all kinds; card index); Certificates of the Treasurer, 10 vols. (for Rev. War service; name lists, badly charred): both series at NYSL; names not printed therefrom.

War Veterans' graves in New York State: abandoned project, done by only a few counties; unorganized results at Bureau of War Records, Albany.

New York Genealogical and Biographical Record, printed quarterly since January 1870 (so much a part of any search that its listing here was overlooked); Subject Index, vols. 1–38 (1907) and Mrs. Barber's MSS Subject Index, vols. 39–76 (1946), and Surname Index, vols. 1–20 (1950).

Index to Genealogical Periodicals, Donald L. Jacobus, 3 vols., 1932, 1948, 1953.

The Columbia Historical Portrait of New York, John A. Kouwenhoven, 1953 (over 900 illustrations; general index & street index).

SUBJECT INDEX

(Italics denote important entries; n, note on page)

MANUSCRIPT, abbreviations key, 61; definition, 67

MAPS, 12 27 35–6 *38–43* 44n 49 59 60 65 77 *78 84*, & indexes, 39

MARRIAGES, church records, *61–4;* city records & indexes, 29 *54 54n 68;* notices, 2 7 *11* 12 13 58 *67 69* 78 *83* 87

MARYLANDERS, 1 *8*

MASONIC LODGES, 14 15 *24* 72

MASONS and bricklayers, 15 17

MASSACHUSETTS people, 1 *8. See also* New Englanders

MECHANICS, 14 15 *20* 24

MEMBERSHIPS. *See* Societies

MERCHANTS, 1 15 *16 17 18* 28 70 *71* 83 88

METHODISTS, *12* 44–5 *62n 62–3* 65

MICHIGANITES, 88

MIDWIVES, 14

MILITARY, NAVAL, and MARINE, 29 *45–8* 52 53 *78–81* 83 *89*; Civil war, 48 78 79–81; lands *re*, 41 47–8 53 86 89; loyalists, 45 47; Mexican war, 47 48 78 79 81; military units, 14 47 79; pensions, bounties, claims (federal & state), 29 45 47–8 53 54 76 78 80 86 89; prisoners, 46 79n 80; Revolutionary war and post-war, 28 41 45 47 48 53–4 76 78 *87* 88 89; Spanish-American war, 81; veterans' and patriotic societies, 14 47 81 88; War of 1812, 45–6 48 54 78

MINISTERS, 11 *12* 14 15 54 *68–9* 83 88

MINNESOTANS, 88

MINORS. *See* Children; Guardians

MONTGOMERY CO., N. Y., 87

MORAVIANS, 44–5 *63*

MORTGAGES. *See* Land

MUSICIANS and musical interests, 14 19 23 28 71

NAMES—changes in, 52 *55*

NAMES—lists of, 16–26 27 30 70–3; by education, 23–4 72; by occupation, 16–22 70–2; by wealth, 25 73; miscellaneous indexes 26 27 30. *See also* City; Directories; Federal; Military; Ministers; State

NATURALISTS, 19. *See also* Sciences

NATURALIZATION, 29 *32–4* 84; indexes, 33

NAVAL and marine. *See* Military

NEGROES, 8 9 15 37 45 59 76 77 80

NEW ENGLANDERS, 1 *8* 14 23 28 29 *30* 72 89. *See also* specific states

NEW JERSEYITES, *8* 10 11 69 75 *87* 89

NEW YORK CITY. *See* City; New Yorkers

NEW YORK COUNTY, 3. *See also* City and county

NEW YORKERS (City), length of residence, 9 29 35 67 84; native, *8* 30 74–5; non-native, 1–2 *8 29–34* 53 56 *67* 71 *74–5* 84. *See also* Removals

NEW YORK STATE RESIDENTS (outside the city), 12 13 22 24 26 29–30 65 69 74 75 83 89; Long Islanders, *8* 31n 77n *86;* upstate and western, *8* 72 *86–7* 86n. *See also* Brooklynites; specific counties; specific records

NEW YORK STATE—official. *See* State

NEWSPAPERS, 30 35 50 *58* 67 75 80 *82 83* 85 88 89; abstracts of notices, 2 *7* 11 27 52 *58* 67 71 87; checklists, 58; subject indexes, 58 83. *See also* Printers and publishers

NORWEGIANS, 31 75

NOTARIES, 13 27 52

NURSES, 14 24

OCCUPATIONAL, compendiums, 17 70 74; directories, 13–15; indexes, 16 17; name lists, 16–24 70–2

OCCUPATIONS, 10 13–15 *16–24* 25 28 29 32 34 35 41 51 55 56 67 *70–2* 76 79 80 84 87 89. *See also* accountants; agriculture and farmers; architects; artists; auctioneers; authors; bankers; booksellers; brokers; builders and building trades; butchers; carpenters; cartmen; coach proprietors; coopers; crafts; credit reporters; dentists; designers; firemen and engineers; grocers; hack-drivers; hairdressers and wig makers; hatters; hospitals; hotel keepers; industries; information offices; insurance; judges; lawyers; leather; manufacturers; masons; mechanics; merchants; midwives; military; ministers; musicians; naturalists; notaries; nurses; physicians and surgeons; policemen; porters; printers and publishers; professions, public officeholders; real estate; saddlers; sciences; seamen; sextons; ship-builders; ship captains; shoemakers and cordwainers; silver and gold smiths; smiths; stage (the); stock brokers; tavern keepers; teachers; tradesmen; transportation; servants

OHIOANS, *75* 80 88

ORANGE CO., N. Y., *8* 10 57

94

SPANISH, 8

STAGE (the), *19* 28 71

STATE, appointments and commissions, 14 *52* 82–3; constitutional requirements, 20–1 25 32 37 52; laws, *52–3*; records, *52–3*; Southern District, 4 6 47. *See also* Courts; Laws; Military; Naturalization; State offices

STATE OFFICES—records of, Adjutant General, 46–8 79 80 *80n* 81; Comptroller, 46 48 89; Health, Dep't. of, 68 86n; Land Office, 41 41n 47 86; N. Y. State Library, *3* 22n *27* 31n 33–4 37 *46–8 52 61* 72 80 86–7 *89*; State, Secretary of, 7 33 41 52 55 86 89; Treasurer, 89; War Records, Bureau of, 89. *See also* Archives—guides to; Courts

STOCK brokers, 18 70

STREETS, naming and location, 15 35 36 *38–43* 49 60 78. *See also* Directories; House; Photographs

SURROGATE. *See* Courts; Probate

SURVEYORS, 39

SWEDENBORGIANS, 64

SWEDES, 8

SWISS, 8 75

TAMMANY, 15 23 *24* 82 84 85

TAVERN KEEPERS, 20

TAX lists and assessments, *25* 37 *43* 50 *73*; Internal Revenue Dep't., 73; valuations (census, etc.), 25 34 37 77

TAX lot numbering, 41

TEACHERS, 14 22 23–4 72

THEATRE. *See* Stage

TRADES. *See* Directories; specific occupations

TRADESMEN, 14 20

TRADE UNIONS and societies. *See* specific occupations

TRANSPORTATION, facilities, 60; men, 17. *See also* Cartmen; Coach proprietors; Hackdrivers; Porters; Seamen; Ship captains

ULSTER CO., N. Y., *8*

UNITARIANS, 64

UNITED STATES. *See* New Englanders; Southerners; Westerners; also specific states

UNIVERSALISTS, 45 61 *64*

VALUATIONS. *See* Tax

VERMONTERS, *8*

VIRGINIANS, 1 *8*

VITAL STATISTICS, 1 8; state, 86n. *See also* Births; Census; Deaths; Life expectancy; Marriages

VOTING, 25 26 37 *84–5*, elected officeholders and candidates, 82; political affiliation of individuals, 26 82 84–5, & of newspapers, 58, 82; political clubs, 85; qualifications, 25 *37*; voters, lists of, 25 *26 36–7* 40 77 *84–5*. *See also* Naturalization; Tammany

WARDS. *See* City—administrative districts

WASHINGTON CO., N. Y., *8*

WASHINGTON, D. C., records at. *See* Federal offices

WEALTH, 17 *25* 26 34 *36–7 73* 77 84; loss of, 83. *See also* Poor

WELSH, 8 *30* 61

WESTCHESTER CO., N. Y., 3n 4n *8* 66n 77n 86n 87

WESTERNERS, 1 86 87–8. *See also* specific states

WEST INDIANS, *8* 45

WIFE and widow, 3 6 7 *11* 13 15 *35* 48 53 55 58 *77* 78

WILLS. *See* Probate

WISCONSINITES, 88

WOMEN'S civic interests, 24 73

GARDEN CITY PRINT, INC.
Newton, Mass.

www.ingramcontent.com/pod-product-compliance
Lightning Source LLC
Chambersburg PA
CBHW070929270326
41927CB00011B/2785